THE GREATEST JOKE COMPENDIUM OF ALL TIME — FOR OUR TIMES

(Definitely non PC version !!)

COMPILED BY ROY VEGA

authorHOUSE™

1663 Liberty Drive, Suite 200
Bloomington, Indiana 47403
(800) 839-8640
www.AuthorHouse.com

This book is a work of fiction. People, places, events, and situations are the product of the author's imagination. Any resemblence to actual persons, living or dead, or historical events, is purely coincidental.

© *2005 COMPILED BY ROY VEGA. All Rights Reserved.*

No part of this book may be reproduced, stored in a retrieval system, or transmitted by any means without the written permission of the author.

First published by AuthorHouse 03/16/05

ISBN: 1-4208-2772-3 (sc)

Printed in the United States of America
Bloomington, Indiana

This book is printed on acid-free paper.

Table of Contents

Children 1
   Why parents get grey hair 1
   Mind your language 2
   Never lie to your mum 3
   Mothers 4

Medical Problems 6
   Gas 6
   Test results 6
   Viagra 7
   The psychiatric hospital 8
   Examinations 9
   Redneck Vasectomy 9
   Brains 10
   Three sick men 11
   Beware Headaches 12
   The queen's visit 13

The WOW Factor 15
   Dave 15

Men on Women 17
   The Ostrich Story 17
   Husband Shopping 23
   Dear Technical Support, ... 24
   Perfection 25
   One Wish 26
   Think Positive 27

Inventions 27
Real Problems Solved 28
The Knob 31

Women on Men 32
Don't upset this lot 32
A poem for us 34
The Wisdom of a Navajo Woman 36
He asked for it 36
Words women use for man's attention 37
Ouch! 39
Translating women's English 42
Orgasms 44
Life is easier for a man 44
Great comebacks 45
15 Pieces of Advice to be Passed on to your Daughters 46
Still not happy! 47
The Rope 49
Babies 49
Blowjobs 50
Why men pee standing 51
Curiosity 51
Doctors – what do they know? 53
Why waste a magic lamp? 53
What every woman knows 54
Just what are they good for? 54
New baby 58
Men Are Like… 59
Are we there yet? 60
The Fairy 60

Men on Men 64
   Men's rules 64
   Let's go drinking 67

Women on women 70
   The Geography of a Woman 70
   The Geography of a Man 71
   Why women like frogs 71
   The advertising codes! 72

Weapons of Mass Destruction 74

Beer Legends 75
   Be Alert - New Health Scare 75
   Late Again 76
   Beer Scooters 77
   Self preservation technique 79
   Heed the warnings 80

Sex jokes – the way it is 82
   Entrepreneurs 82
   Advertising 82
   First time 83
   It's all in the name 83
   Persistence might pay 83
   The pickle slicer 84
   Opportunist 85
   The L0VE Dress 86
   Essex Girls 87
   The revelation 88
   Cowboys 88
   Keith 89
   The Gift 90

Great boss 91
Why Fishing is better than sex: 91
Affairs 93
Parrots 95
Death Grip 96
Sexual Calorie Counter 96
The Penis' Request 98
The Chemists 99
Quick thinking 100
What a gent 101
The seven dwarfs 102
The kinds of sex 104
Husband wanted 104
Voodoo Penis 106
James Bond 108
After the wedding 109
Live on the radio 110
New neighbour 112

Vive La Difference 113
Prayers 114
The truth about men and women 116
Toilet humour 119

Amateur Psychiatry 122
The logical scientist 122

Pets 125
At the vets 125
What an octopus 126
The new pet 127

Regional vibe **128**
　　The cat bronze 128
　　Love those Essex girls 131
　　Perfume 131

The Irish Section! **133**
　　Irish Scarecrow 133
　　Stay clear of technology 133
　　Spanner 134
　　Great bar 135
　　Naming 135
　　Fair cop 136
　　Thank you doctor 136
　　The Leprechaun 138
　　Opportunist 139
　　To see ourselves as others see us 139
　　Don't try this at home 140
　　A tale of two pigs 141
　　The masterpiece 143
　　It's a girl! 143

Consultants **145**
　　Modern day man 145
　　The power of letters 146

The art of Management **149**
　　Management Lessons Lesson One 149
　　Lesson 4 150

Driving **152**
　　Road signs 152

Sexist – plain & simple **163**
　　New cash machines 163

The male view 165
Showering 167
Ergonomic mouse 170
Woman driver 172

Work – Pah! 173
Oops 173
Misunderstanding 174

Parental wisdom 176
Lessons taught by Mum 176
Careful of my daughter! 178

Commentating is not easy you know! 180
Foot in mouth 180

Toilet Humour 183
Good Afternoon 183
Bathroom Scribble - pearls of wisdom from around the world 183

Blonde Jokes 186
Message Centre 186
He's right you know 187
The Mechanic 188
Priceless 188
Flowers 189
Overweight Blonde 189
Exposure 190
River Walk 190
Knitting 190
Blonde on the Sun 191
Speeding Ticket 191
The Vacuum 191

Final Exam 192
The Blonde Joke to End All Blonde Jokes! 192
It's hereditary 193
The Ventriloquist 194

Age 195
Thought for the Day 195
Ethel's Wheelchair 195
Court Appearance 196
You know you are getting old when 197

Commerce 201
Capitalism 201

Cultural Differences 204
Party Invitation 204
Scousers 205
Travel Advice 206
Boozing can be dangerous 210
The desert island 211
Chinese proverbs 213
Hospitals in Scotland 215
Read the label 216
Drinking buddies 218
Top 10 reasons for your nationality 219
Nelson Mandela 225

Questions of Ethics 227
Your choice 227

Celebs 229
Big Sean 229
Sherlock Holmes 230

Philosophy **232**
Cats 232
Dogs 232
Why did the chicken cross the road? 233
Bill G 236
Musings 237
The boy learns! 239
A model for life's meaning. 240

Terror **242**
Warning 242
This boy will go far 243

Religion **244**
Appearances can be deceptive! 244
Spread a little happiness 245
The bible says…… 246
B I G Trouble 247
Ingenuity! 248
Forrest Gump – now he's sharp! 249
An audience with the Pope 251
Be careful what you wish for 251
They really wrote these 252

Brainteasers **258**
Fs 258

Modern Living **259**
You know you are living in the current age when: 259
Boy is he miserable 260
How's your relationship with the bank? 262

Information **267**
    Airlines 267

Ingenuity **273**
    Cancel the crane – we've sorted it 273
    Handsfree 273
    Watch out for this scam 275

Advertising **276**
    A desperate Australian male 276

Natural disasters **277**
    Dudley Earthquake appeal 277
    How to handle an irate customer 278

Answers to those every day questions **280**

Chain Letters **284**
    The First Worthwhile Chain Letter 284

Language **287**
    The F word 287
    Complaints to the Council 288

Footie **291**
    World cup 2006 291
    World Cup 2006 – Squads announced! 292

Dodgy Radio Interviews **298**
    Oz 298

At work **301**
    Bad day at the office! 301
    The teacher 302

Charity **303**
   An appeal 303

Technology **305**
   Wrong email address.. 305

Christmas..**307**
   Do you believe? 307

Pure Genius **309**
   Is Hell exothermic (gives off heat) or endothermic (absorbs heat)? 309
   Maths Exam 310
   Bush reasoning... 313

Kylie **314**
   Alone at last 314

Still Bored?? **316**
   Try This.. 316

Children

Why parents get grey hair

The boss of a big company needed to call one of his employees about an urgent problem with one of the main computers. He dialled the employee's home phone number and was greeted with a child's whispered, "Hello?"

"Is your daddy home?" he asked.

"Yes", whispered the small voice.

"May I talk with him?" To the surprise of the boss, the small voice whispered, "No".

Wanting to talk with an adult, the boss asked, "Is your mommy there?"

"Yes", came the answer.

"May I talk with her?"

Again the small voice whispered, "No." Hoping there was somebody with whom he could leave a message, the boss asked, "Is anybody else there?" the boss asked the child.

"Yes" whispered the child, "a policeman."

Wondering what a cop would be doing at his employee's home, the boss asked, "May I speak with the policeman?"

"No, he's busy," whispered the child.

"Busy doing what?" asked the boss.

"Talking to Daddy and Mommy and the fireman", came the whispered answer.

Growing concerned and even worried as he heard what sounded like a helicopter through the earpiece on the phone the boss asked, "What is that noise?"

"A hello-copper" answered the whispering voice.

"What is going on there?" asked the boss, now alarmed. In a whispering voice the child answered, "The search team just landed the hello-copper."

Alarmed, concerned, and more than just a little frustrated the boss asked, "What are they searching for?"

Still whispering, the young voice replied along with a muffled giggle:

"Me".

Mind your language

A mother was working in the kitchen, listening to her five year old son playing with his new electric train in the living room. She heard the train stop and her son saying, "All of you bastards who want off, get the hell off now, cause this is the last stop! And all of you bastards who are getting on, get your ass in the train, cause we're going down the tracks".

The horrified mother went in and told her son, "We don't use that kind of language in this house. Now I want you to go to your room and stay there for TWO HOURS. When you come out, you may play with your train, but I want you to use nice language."

Two hours later, the son came out of the bedroom and resumed playing with his train. Soon the train stopped and the mother heard her son say, "All passengers who are disembarking the train, please remember to take all of your belongings with you. We thank you for travelling with us today and hope your trip was a pleasant one." She hears the little boy continue, "For those of you just boarding, we ask you to stow all of your hand luggage under your seat. Remember, there is no smoking on the train. We hope you will have a pleasant and relaxing journey with us today." As the mother began to smile, the child added, "For those of you who are pissed off about the TWO HOUR delay, please see the fat bitch in the kitchen."

Never lie to your mum

A young man called John invited his mother over for dinner. During the course of the meal, his mother couldn't help but notice how handsome John's male flatmate was. She had long been suspicious of a relationship between the two, and this only made her more curious.

Over the course of the evening, while watching the two interact, she started to wonder if there was more between John and his flatmate than met the eye. Reading his Mum's thoughts, John volunteered, "I know what you must be thinking, but I assure you, Simon and I are just flatmates."

a week later, Simon came to John saying, "...ce your mother came to dinner I've been ...find the beautiful silver gravy ladle. You don't suppose she took it, do you?" "Well, I doubt it, but I'll email her just to be sure," said John. So he sat down and wrote

Dear Mother,
I'm not saying that you 'did' take the gravy ladle from my house, I'm not saying that you 'did not' take the gravy ladle, but the fact remains that it has been missing ever since you were here for dinner.
Love, John"

Several days later John received an email from his Mother that read:

"Dear Son,
I'm not saying that you 'do' sleep with Simon, I'm not saying that you 'do not' sleep with Simon, but the fact remains that if he was sleeping in his own bed he would have found the gravy ladle by now.
Love, Mum "

Mothers

A young man excitedly tells his mother he's fallen in love and is going to get married.

He says, "Just for fun, Mum, I'm going to bring over 2 other female friends in addition to my fiancée and you try and guess which one I'm going to marry."

The next day, he brings 3 beautiful women into the house, sits them down on the sofa, and they chat for a while. He then says, "Okay, Mum. Guess which one I'm going to marry."

She immediately replies, "The red-head in the middle."

"That's amazing, Mum. You're right, how did you know?"

"I don't like her."

Medical Problems

Gas

This little old lady goes to the doctor and says, "Doctor I have this problem with passing gas, but it really doesn't bother me too much. It never smells and it's always silent. As a matter of fact I've passed gas at least 20 times since I've been here in your office. You didn't know I was passing gas because it doesn't smell and it's silent".

The doctor says "I see. Take these pills and come back to see me next week." The next week the lady goes back. "Doctor," she says, "I don't know what you gave me, but now my passing gas… although still silent, it stinks terribly."

"Good", the doctor said, now that we've cleared up your sinuses, we'll start to work on your hearing.

Test results

A woman is feeling very ill and has a lot of medical tests done to find the cause.

Her husband is asked to go to the surgery the results of the tests. The receptionist says, ' lab aren't too sure about the results, but it's e news or really bad news".

"What's the bad news?", he asks.

"It might be Alzheimers"

"Jeez! That's terrible! What's the *really* bad news?"

"It might be AIDS." says the receptionist.

"Oh No! How can I tell? What can I do?"

"I'll just check with the Doctor", she says.

When she comes back, he asks, "What does the Doctor recommend?"

"Well, he suggests that you take her into town for a slap-up meal. Leave her there. If she finds her own way home, don't Shag her!"

Viagra

A guy falls asleep on the beach for several hours and gets a horrible sunburn. He goes to the hospital and is promptly admitted after being diagnosed with second degree burns.

He was already starting to blister and in agony. The doctor prescribed continuous intravenous feeding with saline and electrolytes, a sedative, and a Viagra pill every four hours.

The nurse, rather astounded, said, "What good will Viagra do him?"

The doctor replied, "It'll keep the sheets off his legs

The psychiatric hospital

Hello, and welcome to the mental health hotline…"

If you are obsessive-compulsive, press 1 repeatedly.

If you are co-dependent, please ask someone to press 2 for you.

If you have multiple personalities, press 3, 4, 5, and 6.

If you are paranoid, we know who you are and what you want. Stay on the line so we can trace your call.

If you are delusional, press 7 and your call will be transferred to the mother ship.

If you are schizophrenic, listen carefully and a small voice will tell you which number to press.

If you are a manic-depressive, it doesn't matter which number you press, no one will answer.

If you are dyslexic, press 9696969696969696.

If you have a nervous disorder, please fidget with the pound key until a representative comes on the line.

If you have amnesia, press 8 and state your name, address, telephone number, date of birth, social security number, and your mother's maiden name.

If you have post-traumatic stress disorder, s-l-o-w-l-y & c-a-r-e-f-u-l-l-y press 0 0 0.

If you have Bi-polar disorder, please leave a message after the beep or before the beep or after the beep. Please wait for the beep.

If you have short-term memory loss, press 9. If you have short-term memory loss, press 9. If you have short-term memory loss, press 9. If you have short-term memory loss, press 9.

If you have low self-esteem, please hang up. All operators are too busy to talk to you."

If you are blonde don't press any buttons, you'll just screw it up.

Examinations

An attractive young girl, chaperoned by an ugly old lady, entered the doctor's office.

"We have come for an examination," said the young girl.

"All right," said the doctor. "Go behind that curtain and take your clothes off."

"No, not me," said the girl. "it's my old aunt here."

"Very well," said the doctor. "Madam, stick out your tongue

Redneck Vasectomy

After having their 11th child, an Alabama couple decided that was enough, as they could not afford a larger bed. So the husband went to his veterinarian and told him that he and his cousin didn't want to have any more children.

The doctor told him that there was a procedure called a vasectomy that could fix the problem but that it was expensive. A less costly alternative, said the doctor, was to go home, get a cherry bomb (fireworks are legal in Alabama), light it, put it in a beer can, then hold the can up to his ear and count to 10. The Alabamian said to the doctor, "I may not be the smartest man in the world, but I don't see how putting a cherry bomb in a beer can next to my ear is going to help me." "Trust me," said the doctor.

So the man went home, lit a cherry bomb and put it in a beer can. He Held the can up to his ear and began to count: "1" "2" "3" "4" "5" At which point he paused, placed the beer can between his legs, and resumed counting on his other hand.

This procedure also works in Kentucky, Mississippi, and West Virginia.

Brains

In the hospital the relatives gathered in the waiting room, where their family member lay gravely ill. Finally, the doctor came in looking tired and sombre.

"I'm afraid I'm the bearer of bad news," he said as he surveyed the worried faces. "The only hope left for your loved one at this time is a brain transplant. It's an experimental procedure, semi-risky and you will have to pay for the brain yourselves."

The family members sat silent as they absorbed the news. After a great length of time, someone asked, "Well, how much does a brain cost?" The doctor quickly responded, "£5,000 for a male brain, and £200 for a female brain."

The moment turned awkward. Men in the room tried not to smile, avoiding eye contact with the women, but some actually smirked.

A man, unable to control his curiosity, blurted out the question everyone wanted to ask, "Why is the male brain so much more?"

The doctor smiled at the childish innocence and so to the entire group said, "It's just standard pricing procedure. We have to mark down the price of the female brains, because they've actually been used."

Three sick men

Three desperately ill men met with their doctor one day to discuss their options. One was an alcoholic, one was a chain smoker, and one was a homosexual. The doctor, addressing all three of them, said, "If any of you indulge in your vices one more time, you will surely die."

The men left the doctor's office, each convinced that he would never again indulge himself in his vice. While walking toward the subway for their return trip to the suburbs, they passed a bar.

The alcoholic, hearing the loud music and seeing the lights, could not stop himself. His buddies accompanied him into the bar, where he had a shot of whiskey. No sooner had he replaced the shot glass on the bar, he fell off his stool, stone cold dead. His companions, somewhat shaken up, left the bar, realizing how seriously they must take the doctor's words.

As they walked along, they came upon a cigarette butt lying on the ground, still burning.

The homosexual looked at the chain smoker and said, "If you bend over to pick that up, we're both dead."

Beware Headaches

Joe was a successful lawyer, but as he got older he was increasingly hampered by incredible headaches. When his career and love life started to suffer, he sought medical help. After being referred from one specialist to another, he finally came across an old country doctor who solved the problem.

"The good news is I can cure your headaches... The bad news is that it will require castration. You have a very rare condition which causes your testicles to press up against the base of your spine and the pressure creates one hell of a headache. The only way to relieve the pressure is to remove the testicles."

Joe was shocked and depressed. He wondered if he has anything to live for. He couldn't concentrate long enough to answer, but decided he had no choice but to go under the knife. When he left the hospital he was without a headache for the first time in 20 years, but he felt like he was missing an important part of himself.

As he walked down the street, he realised that he felt like a different person. He could make a new beginning and live a new life.

He saw a men's clothing store and thought, "That's what I need - a new suit." He entered the shop and told the salesman, "I'd like a new suit." The elderly tailor eyed him briefly and said, "Let's see... size 44 long."

Joe laughed, "That's right, how did you know?"

"Been in the business 60 years!"

Joe tried on the suit. It fit perfectly. As Joe admired himself in the mirror, the salesman asked, "How about a new shirt?" Joe thought for a moment and then said, "Sure…"

The salesman eyed Joe and said, "Let's see… 34 sleeve and… 16 and a half neck."

Joe was surprised, "That's right, how did you know?"

"Been in the business 60 years!"

Joe tried on the shirt, and it fit perfectly. As Joe adjusted the collar in the mirror, the salesman asked, "How about new shoes?"

Joe was on a roll and said, "Sure …"

The salesman eyed Joe's feet and said, "Let's see… 9-1/2…E."

Joe was astonished, "That's right, how did you know?"

"Been in the business 60 years!"

Joe tried on the shoes and they fit perfectly. Joe walked comfortably around the shop and the salesman asked, "How about some new underwear?"

Joe thought for a second and said, "Sure…"

The salesman stepped back, eyed Joe's waist and said, "Let's see…size 36."

Joe laughed, "Ah ha! I got you! I've worn size 34 since I was 18 years old." The salesman shook his head, "You can't wear a size 34. It will press your testicles up against the base of your spine and give you one hell of a headache."

The queen's visit

The Queen was visiting one of London's top hospitals and she specified she wanted to see absolutely

g. During her tour of the floors she passed a ...re a male patient was masturbating.

"Oh my", said the Queen, "that's disgraceful, what is the meaning of this?"

The Doctor leading the tour explains; "I am sorry Your Majesty, but this man has a very serious medical condition and is only following doctors orders. His body produces too much semen and his testicles keep overfilling. Until we can find out exactly what is causing this problem he's been instructed to do that at least 5 times a day or there is a danger that his testicles will explode, and he would die instantly."

"Oh, I am so sorry", said the Queen.

On the next floor they passed a room where a nubile young nurse was giving patient a blowjob "Oh my", said the Queen, "What's happening in there?"

The Doctor replied, "Same problem, but he's with BUPA.

The WOW Factor

Dave

Dave was bragging to his boss one day, "You know, I know everyone there is to know. Just name someone, anyone, and I know them."

Tired of his boasting, his boss called his bluff, "OK, Dave, how about Tom Cruise?" "No drama's boss, Tom and I are old friends and I can prove it."

So Dave and his boss fly out to Hollywood and knock on Tom Cruise's door and Tom Cruise shouts, "Dave! What's happening? Great to see you! Come on in for a beer!"

Although impressed, Dave's boss is still sceptical. After they leave Cruise's house, he tells Dave that he thinks him knowing Cruise was just lucky.

"No, no, just name anyone else," Dave says. "President Bush," his boss quickly retorts. "Yup," Dave says, "Old buddies, let's fly out to Washington." And off they go.

At the White House, Bush spots Dave on the tour and motions him and his boss over, saying, "Dave, what a surprise, I was just on my way to a meeting, but you and your friend come on in and let's have a cup of coffee first and catch up."

Well, the boss is very shaken by now but still not totally convinced.

After they leave the White House grounds he expresses his doubts to Dave, who again implores him to name anyone else.

"The pope," his boss replies. "Sure!" says Dave. "My folks are from Poland, and I've known the Pope a long time."

So off they fly to Rome. Dave and his boss are assembled with the masses in Vatican Square when Dave says, "This will never work. I can't catch the Pope's eye among all these people. Tell you what, I know all the guards so let me just go upstairs and I'll come out on the balcony with the Pope."

And he disappears into the crowd headed toward the Vatican. Sure enough, half an hour later Dave emerges with the Pope on the balcony but by the time Dave returns he finds that his boss has had a heart attack and is surrounded by paramedics.

Working his way to his boss' side, Dave asks him, "What happened?"

His boss looks up and says, "I was doing fine until you and the Pope came out on the balcony and the man next to me said, "Who the fuck's that on the balcony with Dave?"

Men on Women

The Ostrich Story

A man walks into a restaurant with a full-grown ostrich behind him, and as he sits, the waitress comes over and asks for their order.

The man says, "I'll have a hamburger, fries and a coke," and turns to the ostrich.

"What's yours?"

"I'll have the same," says the ostrich. A short time later the waitress returns with the order.

"That will be £7.40 please," and the man reaches into his pocket and pulls out exact change for payment.

The next day, the man and the ostrich come again and the man says, "I'll have a hamburger, fries and a coke," and the ostrich says, "I'll have the same." Once again the man reaches into his pocket and pays with exact change.

This becomes a routine until late one evening, the two enter again. "The usual?" asks the waitress. "No, this is Friday night, so I will have a steak, baked potato and salad," says the man. "Same for me," says the ostrich. A short time later the waitress comes with the order and says, "That will be £21.60." Once again the man pulls exact change out of his pocket and places it on the table. The waitress can't hold back her curiosity any longer.

"Excuse me, sir. How do you manage to always come up with the exact change out of your pocket every time?"

"Well," says the man, "several years ago I was cleaning the attic and I found an old lamp. When I rubbed it a Genie appeared and offered me two wishes. My first wish was that if I ever had to pay for anything, I could just put my hand in my pocket, and the right amount of money would always be there."

"That's brilliant!" says the waitress. "Most people would wish for a million dollars or something, but you'll always be as rich as you want for as long as you live!"

"That's right! Whether it's a gallon of milk or a Rolls Royce, the exact money is always there," says the man.

The waitress asks, "One other thing, sir, what's with the ostrich?"

The man sighs and answers, "My second wish was for a tall bird with long legs who agrees with everything I say!"

Will you women never learn

Dear Ladies,

For too long we men have been divided and conquered in the name of equality, feminism and a host of other bobbins.

THE GREATEST JOKE COMPENDIUM OF ALL TIME — FOR OUR TIMES

No more!

The man fights back!! Tell your friends, the 90's man is dead.... long

live the man of the new millennium.

Listen up ladies; this is how it really is...

If you think you might be fat, you are. Don't ask us. We refuse to answer. Just get your arse down to a gym.

Learn to work the toilet seat: if it's up, just put the bloody thing down. We need it up, you need it down. You don't hear us moaning about you leaving it down.

Don't cut your hair. Ever. It causes unnecessary arguments when we dare to comment on it. Long hair is always more attractive than short hair.

One of the big reasons men fear getting married is that married women always cut their hair.

Birthdays, valentines, and anniversaries are not quests to see if we can find the perfect present... Again.

Sometimes, we're not thinking about you. Live with it.

Saturday is for sport s. It's like the full moon or the changing of the tides so just let it be.

Shopping is not a sport. And no, we are never going to think of it that way.

Anything you wear is fine. Really!!!

Ask for what you want. Let us be clear on this one: subtle hints do not work! Strong hints do not work! Obvious hints do not work! Just tells what you want!

Face it; peeing standing up is more difficult than peeing from point blank range. We're bound to miss sometimes.

Most blokes own two to three pairs of shoes, so what makes you think we'd be any good at choosing which pair, out of thirty, would look good with that particular dress?

'Yes', 'no' and 'mmm' are perfectly acceptable answers.

A headache that lasts for 17 months is a problem. See a doctor.

Your mum doesn't have to be our best friend.

Check your oil and radiator water. It is an essential part of car maintenance.

The relationship is never going to be like it was the first two months we were going out.

Anything we said 6 or 8 months ago is inadmissible in a subsequent argument. In fact, all comments become null and void after 7 days.

It's not the dress that makes you look fat. It's all that bloody chocolate you eat!!

Telling us that the models in the men's magazines are airbrushed makes you sound jealous and petty and it's certainly not going to deter us from reading them.

The male models with great bodies you see in magazines are all gay.

If something we said could be intended two ways, and one of these ways makes you sad and angry, we meant the other one.

THE GREATEST JOKE COMPENDIUM OF ALL TIME — FOR OUR TIMES

Let us ogle. We are going to look anyway; it's genetic. If we don't look at other women, how can we rate how fit you are?

Whenever possible, please say whatever you have to say only during the commercial breaks.

When we are in bed and look tired this means that we are tired and definitely does not mean that we want to discuss the relationship.

If you want some dessert after a meal - have some. You don't have to finish it. You can just taste it if you like but don't say "no, couldn't/shouldn't/don't want any" and then eat half of mine afterwards.

Dieting doesn't work without exercise.

If you're on a diet it doesn't mean my meals should be rabbit food as well.

A man's four essential food groups are: white meat, red meat, good wine and cold lager. Please ensure all meals contain a good balance of the above in acceptable quantities - everything else falls under the category "garnish".

Do not question our sense of direction. If you can learn this, then man and woman can co-exist on a level based on love and mutual respect. Christopher Columbus did not need directions, and neither do we.

Crying is emotional blackmail.

We don't remember dates. Mark birthdays and anniversaries on a calendar. Remind us frequently beforehand.

Come to us with a problem only if you want help solving it. That's what we do. Sympathy is what your girlfriends are for.

You can either ask us to do something or tell us how you want it done. Not both. If you already know best how to do it, just do it yourself.

All men see in only 16 colours, like Windows default settings. Peach, for example, is a fruit, not a colour. We have no idea what mauve is.

If it itches, it will be scratched. We do that. It's genetic.

We are not mind readers and we never will be. Our lack of mind-reading ability is not proof of how little we care about you.

If we ask what is wrong and you say "nothing," we will act like nothing's wrong. We know you are lying, but it is just not worth the hassle getting you to tell us.

If you ask a question you don't want an answer to, expect an answer you don't want to hear.

Don't ask us what we're thinking about unless you are prepared to discuss such topics as computers, football, fluff in your navel, Zen and the art of picking your nose, the 4-4-2 formation or the benefits of drinking real ale.

You have enough clothes, and too many shoes. Yes, you did hear right. Too many shoes!!

Beer is as exciting for us as handbags are for you.

I am in shape. Round is a shape.

The ball is in your court.

Sincerely,

The Lads

Husband Shopping

Recently a "Husband Shopping Centre" opened in Dallas, where women could go to choose a husband from among many men. It was laid out in five floors, with the men increasing in positive attributes as you ascended. The only rule was, once you opened the door to any floor, you HAD to choose a man from that floor. If you went up a floor, you couldn't go back down except to leave the place, never to return.

A couple of girlfriends went to the shopping centre to find some husbands...

First floor

The door had a sign saying, "These men have jobs and love kids". The women read the sign and said, "Well that's better than not having a job, or not loving kids, but I wonder what's further up?" So up they went.

Second floor

The sign read, "These men have high paying jobs, love kids, and are extremely good looking." "Hmmm", said the ladies. "But, I wonder what's further up?"

Third floor

This sign read, "These men have high paying jobs, are extremely good looking, love kids and help with the housework." "Wow!" said the women. "Very tempting, BUT, there's more further up!" And up they went.

Fourth floor

This door had a sign saying "These men have high paying jobs, love kids, are extremely good looking, help with the housework, and have a strong romantic streak." "Oh, mercy me. But just think! What must be awaiting us further on!" So up to the fifth floor they went.

Fifth floor

The sign on that door said, "This floor is empty and exists only to prove that women are bloody impossible to please".

Dear Technical Support,

18 months ago, I upgraded to Girlfriend 1.0 from Drinking Mates 4.2, which I had used for years without any trouble. However, there are apparently conflicts between these two products and the only solution was to try and run Girlfriend 1.0 with the sound turned off. To make matters worse, Girlfriend 1.0 is incompatible with several other applications, such as Lads Night Out 3.1, Football 2.0, and Lapdancing club 6.9. Successive versions of Girlfriend proved no better. A shareware program, Party Girl 2.1, which I tried, had many bugs and left a virus in my system, forcing me to shut down completely for several weeks.

Eventually, I tried to run Girlfriend 1.2 and Girlfriend 1.0 at the same time, only to discover that when these two systems detected each other, they caused severe damage to my hardware.

I then upgraded to Fiancé 1.0, only to discover that this product soon had to be upgraded further to Wife 1.0. While Wife 1.0 tends to use up all my available resources, it does come bundled with FreeSex Plus and Cleanhouse 2002.

Shortly after this upgrade, however, I found that Wife 1.0 could be very unstable and costly to run. Any mistakes I made were automatically stored in Wife 1.0's memory and could not be deleted. They then resurfaced months later when I had forgotten about them. Wife 1.0 can, without warning, launch TurboStrop and Whinge. These latter products have no Help files, and I have to try to guess what the problem is.

Wife 1.0 also spawns unwelcome child processes that drain my resources. These conflict with some of the new games I wanted to try out, like all night drinking session 5.1, warning me that they are an illegal operation.

Wife 1.0 also comes with a rather annoying pop-up called Mother-In-Law, which can't be turned off.

Recently I've been tempted to install Mistress 2003, but there could be problems. A friend of mine has alerted me to the fact that if Wife 1.0 detects Mistress 2003; it tends to delete all of your Money files before uninstalling itself.

Perfection

Once: upon a time, a perfect man and a perfect woman met. After a perfect courtship, they had a perfect wedding.

Their life together was, of course, perfect.

One snowy, stormy Christmas Eve, this perfect couple was driving their perfect car along a winding road, when they noticed someone at the side of the road in distress. Being the perfect couple, they stopped to help.

There stood Santa Claus with a huge bundle of toys. Not wanting to disappoint any children on the eve of Christmas, the perfect couple loaded Santa and his toys into their vehicle. Soon they were driving along delivering the toys.

Unfortunately, the driving conditions deteriorated and the perfect couple; and Santa Claus had an accident. Only one of them survived the accident.

Question: Who was the survivor?

(Scroll down for the answer. Trust me, it's worth it)

Answer:

The perfect woman survived. She's the only one who really existed in the first place. Everyone knows there is no Santa Claus and there is no such thing as a perfect man.

**** Women - stop reading here, that is the end of the joke.

**** Men - keep scrolling.

So, if there is no perfect man and no Santa Claus, the woman must have been driving. This explains why there was a car accident.

****Men - keep scrolling

By the way, if you're a woman and you're still reading, this illustrates another point: Women never listen.

One Wish

A man walking along a California beach was deep in prayer. All of a sudden, he said out loud, "Lord grant me one wish." Suddenly the sky clouded above his head and in a booming voice the Lord said, "Because you have TRIED to be faithful to me in all ways, I will grant you one wish." The man said, "Build a bridge to Hawaii, so I can drive over any time I want to." The Lord said, "Your request is very materialistic.

Think of the logistics of that kind of undertaking. The supports required to reach the bottom of the Pacific! The concrete and steel it would take! I can do it, but it is hard for me to justify your desire for worldly things. Take a little more time and think of another wish, a wish you think would honour and glorify me."

The man thought about it for a long time. Finally he said, "Lord, I wish that I could understand women. I want to know how they feel inside, what they are thinking when they give me the silent treatment, why they cry, what they mean when they say 'nothing', and how I can make a woman truly happy." After a few minutes the Lord said, "You want two lanes or four on that bridge?"

Think Positive

Naked lady stood staring into a mirror.

"I'm fat and I'm ugly," she says.

Turns to her husband and says, "Make me feel better, pay me a compliment".

"There's nothing wrong with your eyesight!"

Inventions

The man discovered WEAPONS and invented HUNTING

The woman discovered HUNTING and invented FURS.

The man discovered COLOURS and invented PAINT,

The woman discovered PAINT and invented MAKEUP.

The man discovered the WORD and invented CONVERSATION,

The woman discovered CONVERSATION and invented GOSSIP.

The man discovered AGRICULTURE and invented FOOD,

The woman discovered FOOD and invented DIET.

The man discovered FRIENDSHIP and invented LOVE,

The woman discovered LOVE and invented MARRIAGE.

The man discovered WOMEN and invented SEX,

The woman discovered SEX and invented HEADACHES.

The man discovered TRADING and invented MONEY,

The woman discovered MONEY and that's when it all got fucked up

Real Problems Solved

Real life. Real problems. Its a real world

Q: My husband wants a threesome with my best friend and me.

A: Obviously your husband cannot get enough of you! Knowing that there is only one of you he can only settle for the next best thing your best fri[end]. [His sexuality] being an issue, this can bring you closer t[ogether. Why] not get one of your old collage roomm[ates involved] too? If you are still apprehensive, mayb[e you should] let him be with your friends without you. [If you are] not sure then just perform oral sex on him and cook him a nice meal while you think about it.

Q: My husband continually asks me to perform oral sex on him.

A: Do it. Semen can help you lose weight and gives a great glow to your skin. Interestingly, men know this. His offer to allow you to perform oral sex on him is totally selfless. This shows he loves you. The best thing to do is to thank him by performing it twice a day; then cook him a nice meal.

Q: My husband has too many nights out with the boys.

A: This is perfectly natural behaviour and it should be encouraged. The Man is a hunter and he needs to prove his prowess with other men. A night out chasing young single girls is a great stress relief and can foster a more peaceful and relaxing home. Remember, nothing can rekindle your relationship better than the man being away for a day or two (it's a great time to clean the house too)! Just look at how emotional and happy he is when he returns to his stable home. The best thing to do when he gets home is for you and your best friend to perform oral sex on him. Then cook

Him a nice meal.

Q: My husband doesn't know where my clitoris is.

A: Your clitoris is of no concern to your husband. If you must mess with it, do it in your own time or ask your best friend to help. You may wish to videotape yourself while doing this, and present it to your husband as a birthday gift. To ease your selfish guilt, perform oral sex on him and cook him a delicious meal.

Q: My husband is uninterested in foreplay.

A: You are a bad person for bringing it up and should seek sensitivity training. Foreplay to a man is very stressful and time consuming. Sex should be available to your husband on demand with no pesky requests for foreplay. What this means is that you do not love your man as much as you should; He should never have to work to get you in the mood. Stop being so selfish! Perhaps you can make it up to him by performing oral sex on him and cooking him a nice meal.

Q: My husband always has an orgasm then rolls over and goes to sleep without giving me one.

A: I'm not sure I understand the problem here. Perhaps you've forgotten to cook him a nice meal.

Remember the Acronym W.I.F.E it only stands for…..Wash……Iron……Fuck……Etc. These are very simple commands; there is no compromise and no complaining. You should be in the kitchen, Cooking.

The Knob

A lady in her late 40's went to a plastic surgeon for a face lift. The doctor told her of a new procedure called "The Knob." This small knob is planted on the back of a woman's head and can be turned to tighten up the skin to produce the effect of a brand new facelift forever. Of course the woman wanted "the Knob."

Fifteen years later the woman went back to the surgeon with 2 problems. "All these years everything had been working just fine. I've had to turn the knob on lots of occasions and I've loved the results. But now, Now I have developed two annoying problems. First of all I have got these terrible bags under my eyes and the knob won't get rid of them "

The doctor looked at her and said, "Those aren't bags, those are your breasts." She replied, "Well, I guess that explains the goatee."

Women on Men

Don't upset this lot

Q. What should you do if you see your ex-husband rolling around in pain on the ground?
A. Shoot him again.

Q. How can you tell when a man is well-hung?
A. When you can just barely slip your finger in between his neck and the noose.

Q. Why do little boys whine?
A. Because they're practicing to be men.

Q. How many men does it take to screw in a light bulb?
A. One - he just holds it up there and waits for the world to revolve around him. OR Three - one to screw in the bulb, and two to listen to him brag about the screwing part.

Q. What do you call a handcuffed man?
A. Trustworthy.

Q. What does it mean when a man is in your bed gasping for breath and calling your name?
A. You didn't hold the pillow down long enough.

Q. Why does it take 100,000,000 sperm to fertilize one egg?
A. Because not one will stop and ask directions.

Q. Why do female black widow spiders kill their males after mating?
A. To stop the snoring before it starts.

Q: Why do men whistle when they're sitting on the toilet?
A: Because it helps them remember which end they need to wipe.

Q: What is the difference between men and women...
A: A woman wants one man to satisfy her every need. A man wants every woman to satisfy his one need.

Q: How does a man keep his youth?
A: By giving her money, furs and diamonds.

Q: How do you keep your husband from reading your e-mail?
A: Rename the mail folder "instruction manuals"

A poem for us.

I shave my legs,
I sit down to pee.
And I can justify
any shopping spree.

Don't go to a barber,
but a beauty salon.
I can get a massage
without a hard-on.

I can balance the checkbook;
I can pump my own gas.
Can talk to my friends,
about the size of my ass.

My beauty's a masterpiece,
and yes, it takes long.
At least I can admit,
to others when I'm wrong.

I don't drive in circles,
at any cost.
And I don't have a problem,
admitting I'm lost.

I never forget,
an important date.
You just gotta deal with it,
I'm usually late.

THE GREATEST JOKE COMPENDIUM OF ALL TIME —
OUR TIME.

I don't watch movies,
with lots of gore.
Don't need instant replay,
to remember the score.

I won't lose my hair,
I don't get jock itch.
And just cause I'm assertive,
Don't call me a bitch.

Don't say to your friends,
Oh yeah, I can get her.
In your dreams, my dear,
I can do better!

Flowers are okay,
But jewellery's best.
Look at me you idiot…
Not at my chest????
I don't have a problem,
With Expressing my feelings.
I know when you're lying,
You look at the ceiling.

DON'T call me a GIRL ,
a BABE or a CHICK .
I am a WOMAN.
Get it?, you DICK!?!

Wisdom of a Navajo Woman

A businesswoman is driving home in northern Arizona when she sees a Navajo woman hitchhiking. Since the trip had been long and quiet, She stops the car and the Navajo woman climbs in.

While making small talk, the Navajo woman glances surreptitiously at a brown bag on the front seat between them.

"If you're wondering what's in the bag," says the business woman,

"It's a bottle of wine. I got it for my husband."

The Navajo woman is silent for a while, nods several times and says thoughtfully ….

"Good trade."

He asked for it

This guy was at home watching the football, when his wife interrupts!

"Could you fix the Fridge door? It won't close properly." she asks.

"Fix the fridge door? Does it look like I have Zanussi written on my forehead? I don't think so".

"Fine!" she says, "Then could you at least fix the steps to the front door? They're about to break."

"Does it look like I've got Ronseal written on my forehead? I don't think so.

I've had enough of this, I'm going down the pub!"

So he goes to the pub and drinks for a couple of hours. When he arrives home, he notices that the steps are fixed.

He goes to the fridge to get a beer and notices that the fridge door is also fixed.

"Honey, how'd this all get fixed?"

"Well" she says, "when you left, I sat outside and cried. Just then a nice and very handsome young man asked me what was wrong, so I told him.

He offered to do all the repairs, and all I had to do was bake him a cake OR have sex with him."

"So, what kind of cake did you bake him?", he asked.

She replied: "HELLO!!!... Do you see Mr. Kipling written on my forehead?

I don't think so!!"

Words women use for man's attention

FINE

This is the word women use to end an argument when they feel they are right and you need to shut up. Never use "fine" to describe how a woman looks - this will cause you to have one of those arguments.

FIVE MINUTES

This is half an hour. It is equivalent to the five minutes that your football game is going to last before you take out the trash, so it's an even trade.

NOTHING

This means "something", and you should be on your toes. "Nothing" is usually used to describe the feeling a woman has of wanting to turn you inside out, upside down, and backwards. 'Nothing" usually signifies an argument that will last "Five Minutes" and end with 'Fine'

GO AHEAD (With Raised Eyebrows)

This is a dare. One that will result in a woman getting upset over "Nothing" and will end with the word "Fine"

GO AHEAD (Normal Eyebrows)

This means "I give up" or "do what you want because I don't care"

You will get a "Raised Eyebrow Go Ahead" in just a few minutes, followed by "Nothing" and "Fine" and she will talk to you in about "Five Minutes" when she cools off.

LOUD SIGH

This is not actually a word, but is a non-verbal statement often misunderstood by men. A "Loud Sigh" means she thinks you are an idiot at that moment, and wonders why she is wasting her time standing here and arguing with you over "Nothing"

SOFT SIGH

Again, not a word, but a non-verbal statement. "Soft Sighs" mean that she is content. Your best bet is to not move or breathe, and she will stay content.

THAT'S OKAY

This is one of the most dangerous statements that a woman can make to a man. "That's Okay," means that she wants to think long and hard before paying you back for whatever it is that you have done. "That's Okay" is often used with the word "Fine" and in conjunction with a "Raised Eyebrow".

GO AHEAD

At some point in the near future, you are going to be in some mighty big trouble.

PLEASE DO

This is not a statement, it is an offer. A woman is giving you the chance to come up with whatever excuse or reason you have for doing whatever it is that you have done. You have a fair chance with the truth, so be careful and you shouldn't get a "That's Okay"

THANKS

A woman is thanking you. Do not faint. Just say you're welcome.

THANKS A LOT

This is much different from "Thanks." A woman will say, "Thanks A Lot" when she is really ticked off at you. It signifies that you have offended her in some callous way, and will be followed by the "Loud Sigh." Be careful not to ask what is wrong after the "Loud Sigh," as she will only tell you "Nothing"

Ouch!

1) He said . . . I don't know why you wear a bra; you've got nothing to put in it.

She said . . . You wear pants don't you?

2) He said . . . Since I first laid eyes on you, I've wanted to make love to you really badly.

She said . . . Well, you succeeded!

3) He said . . .Shall we try swapping positions tonight?

She said . . . That's a good idea - you stand by the ironing board while I sit on the sofa and fart!

4) He said . . . What have you been doing with all the grocery money I gave you? she said. . .Turn sideways and look in the mirror!

5) He said . . . Why don't you tell me when you have an orgasm? she said . . . I would but you're never there.

6) On a wall in a ladies room . . . "My husband follows me everywhere" Written just below it . . . "I do not"

Q. How many honest, intelligent, caring men in the world does it take to do the dishes?
A. Both of them.

Q. Why did the man cross the road?
A. He heard the chicken was a slut.

Q. Why don't women blink during foreplay?
A. They don't have time

Q. What do men and sperm have in common?
A. They both have a one-in-a-million chance of becoming a human being.

Q. How does a man show that he is planning for the future?
A. He buys two cases of beer.

Q. What is the difference between men and government bonds?
A. The bonds mature.

Q. Why are blonde jokes so short?
A. So men can remember them.

Q. How many men does it take to change a roll of toilet paper?
A. We don't know; it has never happened.

Q. Why is it difficult to find men who are sensitive, caring and good-looking?
A. They already have boyfriends.

Q. What do you call a woman who knows where her husband is every night?
A. A widow.

Q. Why are married women heavier than single women?
A. Single women come home, see what's in the fridge and go to bed.
Married women come home, see what's in bed and go to the fridge.

Q. What is the one thing that all men at singles bars have in common?
A. They're married.

Man says to God: "God, why did you make woman so beautiful?"
God says: "So you would love her."
"But God," the man says, "why did you make her so dumb?"
God says: "So she would love you."

Translating women's English

Yes = No
No = Yes
Maybe = No
We need = I want
I'm sorry = You'll be sorry
We need to talk = I need to complain
Sure, go ahead = I don't want you to
Is my bum fat? = Tell me I'm beautiful
Do what you want = You'll pay for this later
I'm not upset = Of course I'm upset, you moron!
Are you listening to me? = Too late, you're dead
You have to learn to communicate = Just agree with me
Be romantic, turn out the lights = I hate my thighs
You're so.. manly = You need a shave and you sweat a lot
Do you love me? = I'm going to ask for something expensive
It's your decision = The correct decision should be obvious by now
You're certainly attentive tonight = Is sex all you ever think about?
I'll be ready in a minute = Kick off your shoes and find a good game on TV
How much do you love me? = I did something today that you're really not going to like

TRANSLATING MEN'S ENGLISH

I'm hungry = I'm hungry

I'm sleepy = I'm sleepy

I'm tired = I'm tired

Nice dress = Nice cleavage!

I love you = Let's have sex now

I'm bored = Do you want to have sex?

What's wrong? = I guess sex tonight is out of the question

I love you too = OK, I said it, can we have sex now?

May I have this dance? = I'd eventually like to have sex with you

Can I call you sometime? = I'd eventually like to have sex with you

Do you want to go to a movie? = I'd eventually like to have sex with you

Can I take you out to dinner? = I'd eventually like to have sex with you

Will you marry me? = I want to make it illegal for you to have sex with other men

You look tense, let me give you a massage = I want to have sex with you in the next 10 minutes

Let's talk = I'm trying to impress you by showing that I a deep person and maybe then you'd like to have sex with me

I don't think those shoes go with that outfit = I'm gay

Orgasms

Life is easier for a man

Your bum is never a factor in a job interview
Your orgasms are always real
Your last name stays put
Nobody secretly wonders if you swallow
Wedding plans take care of themselves
You don't have to curl up next to a hairy bum every night
Foreplay is optional
You never feel compelled to stop a mate from getting shagged
The world is your urinal
Hot wax never comes near your pubic area
Same work, more pay
Car mechanics tell you the truth
Wrinkles add character
You don't have to leave the room to make emergency crotch adjustments
People never glance at your chest when you're talking to them
The occasional well-rendered belch is practically expected
Not liking a person does not preclude having great sex with them
Your mates can be trusted never to trap you with "So, notice anything different"
Going shirtless in public is perfectly acceptable
One mood, all the time….horny

Great comebacks

Man: Haven't I seen you someplace before?
Woman: Yes, that's why I don't go there anymore.

Man: Is this seat empty?
Woman: Yes, and this one will be if you sit down.

Man: Your place or mine?
Woman: Both. You go to yours, and I'll go to mine.

Man: So, what do you do for a living?
Woman: I'm a female impersonator.

Man: Hey baby, what's your sign?
Woman: Do not enter.

Man: How do you like your eggs in the morning?
Woman: Unfertilized.

Man: If I could see you naked, I'd die happy.
Woman: If I saw you naked, I'd probably die laughing.

Man: Your body is like a temple.
Woman: Sorry, there are no services today.

Man: I would go to the end of the world for you.
Woman: But would you stay there?

15 Pieces of Advice to be Passed on to your Daughters

1. Don't imagine you can change a man - unless he's in diapers.
2. What do you do if your boyfriend walks-out? You shut the door.
3. If they put a man on the moon - they should be able to put them all up there.
4. Never let your man's mind wander - it's too little to be out alone.
5. Go for younger men. You might as well - they never mature anyway.
6. Men are all the same - they just have different faces, so that you can tell them apart.
7. Definition of a bachelor; a man who has missed the opportunity to make some woman miserable.
8. Women don't make fools of men - most of them are the do-it-yourself types.
9. Best way to get a man to do something, is to suggest he is too old for it.
10. Love is blind, but marriage is a real eye-opener.
11. If you want a committed man, look in a mental hospital.
12. The children of Israel wandered around the desert for 40 years. Even in biblical times, men wouldn't ask for directions.
13. If he asks what sort of books you're interested in, tell him chequebooks.
14. Remember a sense of humour does not mean that you tell him jokes, it means that you laugh at his.

15. Sadly, all men are created equal.

Still not happy!

Q. What should you do if you see your ex-husband rolling around in pain on the ground?
A. Shoot him again.

Q. How can you tell when a man is well-hung?
A. When you can just barely slip your finger in between his neck and the noose.

Q. Why do little boys whine?
A. Because they're practicing to be men.

Q. How many men does it take to screw in a light bulb?
A. One - he just holds it up there and waits for the world to revolve around him. OR Three - one to screw in the bulb, and two to listen to him brag about the screwing part.

Q. What do you call a handcuffed man?
A. Trustworthy.

Q. What does it mean when a man is in your bed gasping for breath and calling your name?
A. You didn't hold the pillow down long enough.

Q. Why do men name their penises?
A. Because they don't like the idea of having a stranger make 90% of their decisions.

Q. Why does it take 100,000,000 sperm to fertilize one egg?
A. Because not one will stop and ask directions.

Q. Why do female black widow spiders kill their males after mating?
A. To stop the snoring before it starts.

Q: What's the best way to kill a man?
A: Put a naked woman and a six-pack in front of him. Then tell him to pick only one.

Q: What do men and pantyhose have in common?
A: They either cling, run or don't fit right in the crotch!

Q: Why do men whistle when they're sitting on the toilet?
A: Because it helps them remember which end they need to wipe.

Q: What is the difference between men and women...
A: A woman wants one man to satisfy her every need. A man wants every woman to satisfy his one need.

Q: How does a man keep his youth?
A: By giving her money, furs and diamonds.

Q: How do you keep your husband from reading your e-mail?

A: Rename the mail folder to "instruction manuals"

The Rope

There were 11 people hanging onto a rope that came down from a helicopter. Ten were men and one woman.

They all decided that one person should get off, because if they didn't, the rope would break and everyone would die. No one could decide who should go. Finally, the woman gave a really touching speech saying how she would give up her life to save the others, because women were used to giving up things for their husbands and children, giving into men, and not receiving anything in return.

When she finished speaking, all the men started clapping.

Never underestimate the power of a Woman.

Babies

One afternoon a little girl returned from school, and announced that her friend had told her where babies come from.

Amused, her mother replied: "Really, sweetie, why don't you tell me
All about it?"

The little girl explained, "Well... OK... the Mummy and Daddy take off all of their clothes, and the Daddy's thingee sort of stands up, and then Mummy puts it in and then it sort of explodes, and that's how..."

...shook her head, leaned over to meet her, eye to eye and said: "Oh, Darling, that's sweet, but that's not how you get babies. That's how you get jewellery."

Blowjobs

A woman went into a store to buy her husband a pet for his birthday.

After looking around, she found that all the pets were very expensive. She told the clerk she wanted to buy a pet, but she didn't want to spend a fortune.

"Well," said the clerk, "I have a very large bullfrog — they say it's been trained to do blowjobs."

"Blowjobs?", the woman replied.

"It hasn't been proven…but we've sold 30 of them this month," he said. The woman thought it would be a great gag gift and if it's true… no more blowjobs for her! She bought the frog.

When she explained froggy's ability to her husband, he was extremely sceptical and laughed it off. The woman went to bed happy, thinking she may never need to perform this less than riveting act again. In the middle of the night, she was awakened by the noise of pots and pans flying everywhere, making hellish banging and crashing sounds. She ran downstairs to the kitchen, only to find her husband and the frog reading cookbooks.

"What are you two doing at this hour?" she asked.

The husband replied, "If I can teach this frog to cook, you're outta here."

Why men pee standing

Seems God was just about done with creating the universe but he had two extra things left over in his bag so he decided to split them between Adam and Eve. He told them that one of the things he had left was a thing that would allow the owner to pee while standing up. "It's a very handy thing,"

God told them, "and I was wondering if either one of you would like that." Well, Adam jumped up and down and begged "Oh, give that to me! I'd love to be able to do that. It seems just the sort of thing a man should be able to do. Please. Please! Pleeease! Give it to me." On and on he went like an excited little boy.

So Eve just smiled and told God that if Adam really wanted it so badly, he should have it. So God gave Adam the thing that allowed him to pee while standing up and he was so excited. He whizzed on the bark of a tree and then went off to write his name in the sand, laughing with delight all the while.

God and Eve watched him for a moment and then God said to Eve, "Well, here's the other thing and I guess you can have it." "What's it called? Eve asked. "Brains" God said

Curiosity

A man travelling by plane was in urgent need of a restroom, but each time he tried, it was occupied. The flight attendant, aware of his predicament, suggested he use the attendants ladies room, but cautioned him not to press any of the buttons.

There next to the paper roll were four buttons marked respectively: WW, WA, PP, and ATR. Making the mistake so many men make of not listening to a woman, he disregarded what she said when his curiosity got the best of him. He carefully pressed the WW button and immediately a1 gently flush of Warm Water sprayed his bare bottom.

He thought, "Wow, these gals really have it nice." So, a little more boldly he pressed the WA button; Body temperature Warm Air blew across his wet bottom and dried it comfortably.

"Aha," he thought, "No wonder these women take so long in the bathroom with this kind of service! "

So he pushed the next button, PP, with anticipation. A soft disposable Powder Puff swung below him and dusted his bottom lightly with talc. "Man, this is great," he thought as he reached out for the ATR button.

When he awoke in the hospital, the morphine was just wearing off, so in confusion, he buzzed the nurse to find out where he was and what happened. He explained the last thing he remembered was intense pain in the ladies room on the plane.

The nurse explained, "Yes, you must have been having the time of your life until you pushed the Automatic Tampon Removal button. By the way, your penis is under your pillow. "

Doctors – what do they know?

A woman accompanied her husband to the doctor's office. After his check-up, the doctor called the wife into his office alone. He said, "Your husband is suffering from a very severe disease, combined with horrible stress. If you don't do the following, your husband will surely die." "Each morning, fix him a healthy breakfast. Be pleasant, and make sure he is in a good mood. For lunch make him a nutritious meal. For dinner prepare an especially nice meal for him. Don't burden him with chores, as he probably had a hard day. Don't discuss your problems with him, it will only make his stress worse. And most importantly. make love with your husband several times a week and satisfy his every whim." If you can do this for the next 10 months to a year, I think your husband will regain his health completely. On the way home, the husband asked his wife. "What did the doctor say?" "You're going to die," she replied.

Why waste a magic lamp?

One day three guys were out walking, and they found a lamp. So, they rubbed the lamp and a genie popped out. He says "I'll grant you each one wish." These guys weren't so bright, so they all wanted to be smarter. The first guy says "I wish I was 10 times smarter." The genie says "POOF! You're 10 times smarter." The second guy says "I wish to be 100 times smarter." and the genie says "POOF! You're 100 times smarter." The last guy says "I wish to be 1000 times smarter" And the genie says "POOF!! You're a woman!!"

What every woman knows

In the Hospital the relatives gathered in the waiting room, where their family member lay gravely ill. Finally, the doctor came in looking tired and sombre. "I'm afraid I am the bearer of bad news" she said as she surveyed the worried faces, "The only hope left for your loved one at this time is a brain transplant.

It's an experimental procedure, semi-risky, and you will have to pay for the brain yourselves." The family members sat silent as they absorbed the news. After a length of time, someone asked, "Well, how much does a brain cost?"

The doctor quickly responded, "£5000 for a male brain, and £200 for a female brain." The moment turned awkward. Men in the room tried not to smile, avoiding eye contact with the women, but some actually smirked. A man, unable to control his curiosity, blurted out the question everyone wanted to ask, "Why is the male brain so much more?" The doctor smiled at the childish innocence and then to the entire group said, "It's just standard pricing procedure. We have to mark down the price of the female brains, because they've been used."

Just what are they good for?

Why don't women blink during foreplay?
They don't have time.

Why did God put men on earth?
Because a vibrator can't mow the lawn.

Why don't women have men's brains?
Because they don't have penises to keep them in.

What is the insensitive bit at the base of the penis called?
The man.

What's the difference between government bonds and men?
Bonds mature.

What's the difference between a man and E.T.?
E.T. phoned home.

How are men like noodles?
They're always in hot water, they lack taste, and they need dough.

Why do men like BMWs?
They can spell it.

What do a vagina, an anniversary, and a toilet have in common?
Men always miss them.

Why are men like popcorn?
They satisfy you, but only for a little while.

Why are men and spray paint alike?
One squeeze and they're all over you.

Why are men like blenders?
You need one, but you're not quite sure why.

Why is food better than men?
Because you don't have to wait an hour for seconds.

Why do so many women fake orgasm?
Because so many men fake foreplay.

Why do men like frozen microwave dinners so much?
They like being able to both eat and make love in under 5 minutes.

Why would women be better off if men treated them like cars?
At least then they would get a little attention every 6 months or
50,000 miles, whichever came first.

How many men does it take to screw in a light bulb?
One, men will screw anything.

Why do men have a hole in their penis?
So oxygen can get to their brains.

What is the difference between men and pigs?
Pigs don't turn into men when they drink.

What do ceramic tile and men have in common?
If you lay them right the first time, you can walk on them for life!

What is the thinnest book in the world?
What men know about women.

How are men and parking spots alike?
The good ones are always taken and the ones left are handicapped.

What does a man consider a seven course meal?
A hot dog and a six pack of beer.

What's the difference between getting a divorce and getting circumcised?
When you get a divorce, you get rid of the whole prick!

A woman of 35 thinks of having children. What does a man of 35 think of?
Dating children.

What's the difference between a G-Spot and a golf ball?
A guy will actually search for a golf ball.

Why does a bride smile when she walks up the aisle?
She knows she's given her last blow job.

The three words most hated by men during sex?
"Are you In?" or "Is It In?"

Why do men take showers instead of baths?
Pissing in the bath is disgusting.

Three words women hate to hear when having sex?
"Honey, I'm home!"

New baby

A woman gives birth to a baby, and afterwards, the doctor comes in, and he says, "I have to tell you something about your baby."

The woman sits up in bed and says, "What's wrong with my baby, Doctor? What's wrong???"

The doctor says, "Well, now, nothing's wrong, exactly, but your baby is a little bit different. Your baby is a hermaphrodite." The woman says, "A hermaphrodite… what's that???" The doctor says, "Well, it means your baby has the…er…features…of a male and a female."

The woman turns pale. She says, "Oh my god! You mean it has a penis…AND a brain?"

Men Are Like…

Men are like… place mats. They only show up when there's food on the table.

Men are like… mascara. They usually run at the first sign of emotion.

Men are like… bike helmets. Handy in an emergency, but otherwise they just look silly.

Men are like… government bonds. They take so long to mature.

Men are like… parking spots. All the good ones are taken.

Men are like… copiers. You need them for reproduction, but that's about it.

Men are like… lava lamps. Fun to look at, but not all that bright.

Men are like… bank accounts. Without a lot of money, they don't generate much interest.

Men are like… high heels. They're easy to walk on once you get the hang of it.

Men are like… miniskirts. If you're not careful, they'll creep up your legs.

Are we there yet?

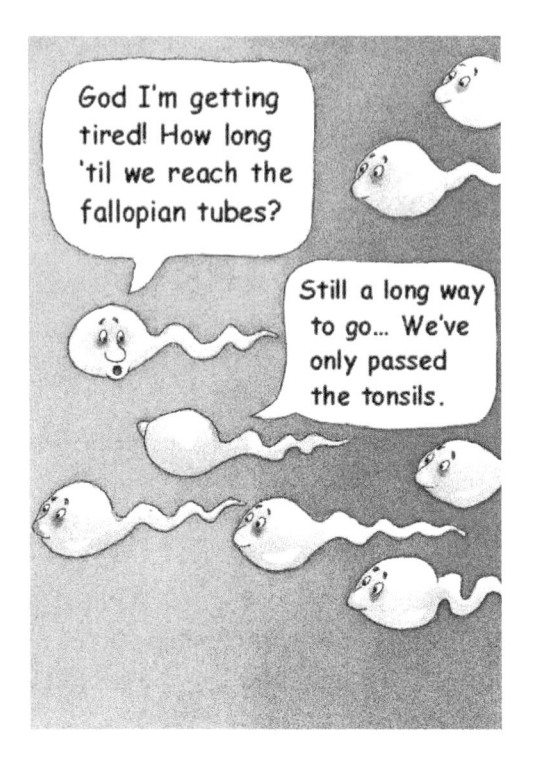

> God I'm getting tired! How long 'til we reach the fallopian tubes?

> Still a long way to go... We've only passed the tonsils.

The Fairy

A couple had been married for 25 years and had also just celebrated their 60th birthdays.

During the celebration a fairy appeared and said that because they had been such a loving couple all those years, she would give them one wish each.

The wife wanted to travel around the world.

The fairy waved her wand and poof...

She had the tickets in her hand.

Next, it was the husband's turn. He paused for a moment, then said, "Well, I'd like to have a woman 30 years younger than me."

The fairy picked up her wand and poof…

He was 90…

All men are bastards but at least the fairies are on our side……

Men on Men

Men's rules

The official 2003 men's rules guide taken from the secret men's handbook

1. Any Man who brings a camera to a stag night may be legally killed by his mates.

2. Under no circumstances may two men share an umbrella.

3. It is ok for a man to cry under the following circumstances:

a. When a heroic dog dies to save its master.

b. The moment Angelina Jolie starts unbuttoning her blouse.

c. After wrecking your boss' car.

d. One hour, 12 minutes, 37 seconds into "The Crying Game".

e. When she is using her teeth.

4. Unless he murdered someone in your family, you must bail a friend out of jail within 12 hours.

5. If you've known a bloke for more than 24 hours, his sister is off limits forever, unless you actually marry her.

6. Moaning about the brand of free beer in a mate's fridge is forbidden. Complain at will if the temperature is unsuitable.

7. No man shall ever be required to buy a birthday present for another man. In fact, even remembering your mate's birthday is strictly optional.

8. On a road trip, the strongest bladder determines pit stops, not the weakest.

9. When stumbling upon other blokes watching a sporting event, you may ask the score of the game in progress, but you may never ask who's playing.

10. You may be flatulent in front of a woman only after you have brought her to climax. If you trap her head under the covers for the purpose of flatulent entertainment, she's officially your girlfriend.

11. It is permissible to quaff a fruity alcopop drink only when you're sunning on a tropical beach… and it's delivered by a topless supermodel…and it's free.

12. Only in situations of Moral and/or physical peril are you allowed to kick another bloke in the nuts.

13. Unless you're in prison, never fight naked.

14. Friends don't let friends wear Speedos. Ever. Issue closed.

15. If a man's fly is down, that's his problem, you didn't see anything.

16. Women who claim they "love to watch sports" must be treated as spies until they demonstrate

knowledge of the game and the ability to drink as much as the other sports watchers.

17. You must offer heartfelt and public condolences over the death of a girlfriend's cat, even if it was you who secretly set it on fire and threw it into a ceiling fan.

18. A man in the company of a hot, suggestively dressed woman must remain sober enough to fight.

19. Never hesitate to reach for the last beer or the last slice of pizza, but not both - that's just mean.

20. If you compliment a bloke on his six-pack, you'd better be talking about his choice of beer.

21. Never join your girlfriend or wife in dissing a Mate of yours, except if she's withholding sex pending your response.

22. Phrases that may not be uttered to another man while lifting weights:

a. Yeah, Baby, Push it!

b. C'mon, give me one more! Harder!

c. Another set and we can hit the showers!

23. Never talk to a man in a bathroom unless you are on equal footing: Both urinating, both waiting in line, etc. For all other situations, an almost imperceptible nod is all the conversation you need.

24. Never allow a telephone conversation with a woman to go on longer than you are able to have sex with her. Keep a stopwatch by the phone. Hang up if necessary.

25. You cannot grass on a colleague who shows up at work with a massive hangover. You may however, hide the aspirin, smear his chair with cheese, turn

the brightness dial all the way down so he thinks his monitor is broken, and have him paged over the loud speaker every seven minutes.

26. The morning after you and a girl who was formerly "just a friend" have carnal drunken monkey sex, the fact that you're feeling weird and guilty is no reason not to nail her again before the discussion about what a big mistake it was.

27. It is acceptable for you to drive her car. It is not acceptable for her to drive yours.

28. Thou shalt not buy a car with an engine capacity of less than 1.5 litres. Thou shall not really buy a car with less than 1.8 litres, 16 valves, and a turbo.

29. Thou shalt not buy a car in the colours of brown, pink, lime green, orange or sky blue.

1. The girl who replies to the question "What do you want for Christmas?" with "If you loved me, you'd know what I want!" gets a Playstation 2. End of story

Let's go drinking

Gentleman's quiz

1. In the company of feminists, coitus should be referred to as:

a) Lovemaking
b) Screwing
c) The pigskin bus pulling into tuna town

2. You should make love to a woman for the first time only after you've both shared:

a) Your views about what you expect from a sexual relationship

b) Your blood-test results
c) Five tequila slammers

3. You time your orgasm so that:
a) Your partner climaxes first
b) You both climax simultaneously
c) You don't miss Sports Centre (Sky)

4. Passionate, spontaneous sex on the kitchen floor is:
a) Healthy, creative love-play
b) Not the sort of thing your wife/girlfriend would ever agree to
c) Not the sort of thing your wife/girlfriend need ever find out about

5. Spending the whole night cuddling a woman you've just had sex with is:
a) The best part of the experience
b) The second best part of the experience
c) $100 extra

6. Your girlfriend says she's gained five pounds in weight in the last month. You tell her that it is:
a) Not a concern of yours
b) Not a problem - she can join your gym
c) A conservative estimate

7. You think today's sensitive, caring man is:
a) A myth
b) An oxymoron
c) A moron

8. Foreplay is to sex as:
a) Appetizer is to entree
b) Priming is to painting
c) A queue is to an amusement park ride

9. Which of the following are you most likely to find yourself saying at the end of a relationship?
a) "I hope we can still be friends."
b) "I'm not in right now. Please leave a message after the tone…."
c) "Welcome to Dumpsville. Population: You."

10. A woman who is uncomfortable watching you masturbate:
a) Probably needs a little more time before she can cope with that sort of intimacy
b) Is uptight and a waste of time
c) Shouldn't have sat next to you on the bus in the first place

If you answered 'A' more than 7 times, check your pants to make sure you really are a man.

If you answered 'B' more than 7 times, check into therapy, you're still a little confused.

If you answered 'C' more than 7 times, call me up. Let's go drinking.

Women on women

The Geography of a Woman

Between 18 and 20 a woman is like Africa, half discovered, half wild, naturally beautiful with fertile deltas.

Between 21 and 30 a woman is like America, well developed and open to trade, especially for someone with cash.

Between 31 and 35 she is like India, very hot, relaxed and convinced of her own beauty.

Between 36 and 40 a woman is like France.. Gently aging but still a warm and desirable place to visit.

Between 41 and 50 she is like Yugoslavia.. Lost the war, haunted by past mistakes — massive reconstruction is now necessary.

Between 51 and 60, she is like Russia, very wide and borders are unpatrolled. The frigid climate keeps people away.

Between 61 and 70, a woman is like Mongolia, with a glorious and all conquering past but alas, no future.

After 70, a woman is like Afghanistan. Most everyone knows where it is, but no one wants to go there.

The Geography of a Man

Between 15 and 70 a man is like Iraq — ruled by a dick.

Why women like frogs

A woman was out golfing one day when she hit her ball into the woods. She went into the woods to look for it and found a frog in a trap.

The frog said to her, "If you release me from this trap, I will grant you 3 wishes." The woman freed the frog.

The frog said, "Thank you, but I failed to mention that there was a condition to your wishes-that whatever you wish for, your husband will get 10 times more or better!"

The woman said, "That would be okay." For her first wish, she wanted to be the most beautiful woman in the world. The frog warned her, "You do realize that this wish will also make your husband the most handsome man in the world, an Adonis, that women will flock to."

The woman replied, "That will be okay because I will be the most beautiful woman and he will only have eyes for me." So, KAZAM - she's the most beautiful woman in the world! For her Second wish, she wanted to be the richest woman in the world. The frog said,

"That will make your husband the richest man in the world and he will be ten times richer than you."

The woman said, "That will be okay because what's mine is his and what's his is mine." So, KAZAM she's the richest woman in the world!

The frog then inquired about her third wish, and she answered, "I'd like a very mild heart attack."

Moral of the story: Women are clever bitches. Don't mess with them

The advertising codes!

* 40-ish……………… 49
* Adventurous…………Slept with all your mates
* Athletic……………..No tits
* Average looking…… Has a face like an arse
* Beautiful…………… Pathological liar
* Contagious Smile……Does a lot of pills
* Educated…………… Was fucked to bits at Uni'
* Emotionally Secure….On medication
* Feminist……………..Fat
* Free spirit…………..Junkie
* Friendship first………Former slut
* Fun…………………..Annoying
* Gentle……………….Dull
* Good Listener………Autistic
* New-Age……………Body hair problems
* Old-fashioned………No BJs or anal
* Open-minded……… Desperate
* Outgoing……………Loud and Embarrassing
* Passionate…………..Sloppy drunk
* Poet………………….Depressive

* Professional............Bitch
* Romantic...............Frigid
* Social..................Fanny like a clowns pocket
* Voluptuous............Very Fat
* Large lady............ Hugely Fat
* Wants Soulmate......Stalker
* Widow.............. Murderer

Weapons of Mass Destruction

Breaking news - Tony Blair is sending the people who chose Liverpool as European Capital of Culture for 2008 to Iraq. He says that if they can find culture in Liverpool, then locating weapons of mass destruction should be a simple task.

Beer Legends

Be Alert - New Health Scare

The World Health Organisation (WHO) has just issued an urgent warning about BARS, (Beer & Alcohol Requirement Syndrome). A newly identified problem has spread rapidly throughout the world. The disease, identified as BARS, affects people of many different ages.

Believed to have started in Ireland in 1500 BC, the disease seems to affect people who congregate in Pubs and Taverns or who just congregate. It is not known how the disease is transmitted but approximately three billion people world-wide are affected, with thousands of new cases appearing every day.

Early symptoms of the disease include an uncontrollable urge at 5:00pm to consume a beer or alcoholic beverage. This urge is most keenly felt on Fridays. More advanced symptoms of the disease include talking loudly, singing off-key, aggression, heightened sexual attraction/confidence, uncalled for laughter, uncontrollable dancing and unprovoked arguing.

In the final stages of the disease, victims are often cross-eyed, and speak incoherently. Vomiting, loss of memory, loss of balance, and loss of clothing can also occur.

Sometimes death ensues, usually accompanied by the victim shouting, "Hey Fred, bet you can't do this!" or "Wanna see how fast it goes??" If you develop any of these symptoms, it is important that you quarantine yourself in a pub with fellow victims until last call or all the symptoms have passed. Sadly, it is reported that the disease can reappear at very short notice or at the latest, on the following Friday. Side effects for survivors include bruising, broken limbs, lost property, killer headaches and divorce. On the up side, there is not, and probably never will be, a permanent cure.

Late Again

The other night I was invited out for a night with the boys. I told my girlfriend that I would be home by midnight… "promise!" Well, the hours passed quickly and the beer was going down way too easy. At 2am, drunk as a skunk, I headed for home. Just as I got in the door, the cuckoo clock in the hall started up and cuckooed three times.

Quickly, I realized she'd probably wake up, so I cuckooed another 9 times. I was really proud of myself for having such a rapid, witty solution, even when smashed, to escape a possible conflict.

The next morning my girlfriend asked me what time I got in, and I told her 12 o'clock. She didn't seem disturbed at all. Got away with that one, I thought! Then she told me we needed a new cuckoo clock. When I asked her why she said, "Well, last night it cuckooed 3 times, then said, 'oh f*ck,' cuckooed 4 more times, cleared its throat, cuckooed another 3 times, giggled, cuckooed twice more…. then farted."

Beer Scooters

Sound Familiar?

This has answered a question I'm sure we have all puzzled over more than once in our lives…..

How many times have you woken up in the morning after a hard night drinking and thought 'How on earth did I get home?' As hard as you try, you cannot piece together your return journey from the pub to your house. The answer to this puzzle is that you used a Beer Scooter. The Beer Scooter is a mythical form of transport, owned and leased to the drunk by Bacchus the Roman god of wine. Bacchus has branched out since the decrease in the worship of the Roman Pantheon and has bought a large batch of these magical devices. The Beer Scooter works in the following fashion: -

The passenger reaches a certain level of drunkenness and the "slurring gland" begins to give off a pheromone. Bacchus or one of his many sub-contractors detects this pheromone and sends down a winged Beer Scooter. The scooter scoops up the passenger and deposits them in their bedroom via a Trans-Dimensional Portal. This is not cheap to run, so a large portion of the passenger's in-pocket cash is taken as payment. This answers the second question after a night out 'How did I spend so much money?'

Unfortunately, Beer Scooters have a poor safety record and are thought to be responsible for over 90% of all UDI (Unidentified Drinking Injuries).

An undocumented feature of the beer scooter is the destruction of time segments during the trip. The nature of Trans-Dimensional Portals dictates that time will be lost, seemingly unaccounted for. This answers a third question after a night out 'What the hell happened?' With good intentions, Bacchus opted for the REMIT (Removal of Embarrassing Moments In Time) add on, that automatically removes, in descending order, those embarrassing parts in time. One person's REMIT is not necessarily the REMIT of another and quite a lot of lost time can be regained in discussions over a period of time.

Independent studies have also shown that Beer Goggles often cause the scooter's navigation system to malfunction thus sending the passenger to a "new" toilet in the home, often with horrific consequences. With recent models including a GPS, Bacchus made an investment in a scooter drive-thru chain specialising in half eaten kebabs and pizza crusts. Another question answered!!

For the family man, Beer Scooters come equipped with flowers picked from other people's garden and Thump-A-Lot boots (Patent Pending). These boots are designed in such a way that no matter how quietly you tip-toe up the stairs, you are sure to wake up your other half. Special anti-gravity springs ensure that you bump into every wall in the house and the CTSGS (Coffee Table Seeking Guidance System) explains the bruised shins.

The final add-on Bacchus saw fit to invest in for some scooters is the TAS (Tobacco Absorption System). This explains how one person can apparently get through 260 Marlboro Lights in a single night.

PS: Don't forget the on-board heater, which allows you to comfortably get home from the pub in sub-zero temperatures, wearing just a T-shirt.

Note: The beer scooter has no link to the beer bus, you know, the one that comes by when you're in the bog after your 10th pint and whisks away all the mingers and replaces them with stunners?

Self preservation technique

Two buddies, Tony and Steve, are getting very drunk at a bar when suddenly Steve throws up all over himself. "Oh no, now Christine will kill me!"

Tony says, "Don't worry, pal. Just tuck a twenty in your breast pocket, tell her that someone threw up on you and gave you twenty dollars for the dry cleaning bill."

So they stay for another couple of hours and get even drunker. Eventually Steve rolls into home and his Christine starts to give him a bad time. "You reek of alcohol and you've puked all over yourself? My God, you're disgusting!"

Speaking very carefully so as not to slur, Steve says, "Nowainaminit,

Can e'splain everthing! Itsh snot wa jew think. I only had a cupla drrinks. But thiss other guy got ssick on me…..he had one too many and he juss couldin hold hizz liquor. He said he was verry sorry an' gave me twennie bucks for the cleaning bill!" Jane looks in the breast pocket and says, "But this is forty bucks." :

"Oh yeah….I almos' fergot, he shhhit in my pants too"

Heed the warnings

New Warnings on Alcoholic Beverages

Due to increasing product liability litigation, American beer Brewers have accepted the FDA's suggestion that the following warning labels be place immediately on all beer containers:

WARNING: The consumption of alcohol may leave you wondering what the hell happened to your bra.

WARNING: The consumption of alcohol may make you think you are whispering when you are not.

WARNING: The consumption of alcohol is a major factor in dancing like a retarded baboon.

WARNING: The consumption of alcohol may cause you to tell your friends over and over again that you love them.

WARNING: The consumption of alcohol may cause you to think you can sing.

WARNING: The consumption of alcohol may lead you to believe that ex-lovers are really dying for you to telephone them at four in the morning.

WARNING: The consumption of alcohol may make you think you can logically converse with members of the opposite sex without spitting.

WARNING: The consumption of alcohol may make you think you have mystical Kung Fu powers, resulting in you getting your ass kicked.

WARNING: The consumption of alcohol may cause you to roll over in the morning and see something really scary.

WARNING: The consumption of alcohol is the leading cause of inexplicable rug burns on the forehead.

WARNING: The consumption of alcohol may create the illusion that you are tougher, smarter, faster and better looking than most people.

WARNING: The consumption of alcohol may lead you to believe you are invisible.

WARNING: The consumption of alcohol may lead you to think people are laughing WITH you.

WARNING: The consumption of alcohol may cause a disturbance in the time-space continuum, whereby gaps of time may seem to literally disappear.

Sex jokes – the way it is

Entrepreneurs

A boy and his date were parked on a back road some distance from town, doing what boys and girls do on back roads some distance from town. Things were getting hot and heavy when the girl stopped the boy. "I really should have mentioned this earlier, but I'm actually a prostitute and I charge £20 for sex," she said. The boy just looked at her for a couple of seconds, but then reluctantly paid her, and they did their thing. After the cigarette, the boy just sat in the driver's seat looking out the window. "Why aren't we going anywhere?" asked the girl. "Well, I should have mentioned this before, but I'm actually a taxi driver, and the fare back to town is £25!"

Advertising

A man is in a hotel lobby. He wants to ask the clerk a question. As he turns to go to the front desk, he accidentally bumps into a woman beside him and as he does, his elbow goes into her breast. They are both startled and he says, "Ma'am, if your heart is as soft as your breast, I know you'll forgive me." She replies, "If your penis is as hard as your elbow, I'm in room 1221."

First time

A young man walks up and sits down at the bar. "What can I get you?" the bartender inquires. "I want 6 shots of Jagermeister," responded the young man. "6 shots?!? Are you celebrating something?" "Yeah, my first blowjob." "Well, in that case, let me give you a 7th on the house." "No offence, sir. But if 6 shots won't get rid of the taste, nothing will."

It's all in the name

A businessman boards a flight and is lucky enough to be seated next to an absolutely gorgeous woman. They exchange brief hellos and he notices she is reading a manual about sexual statistics. He asks her about it and she replies, "This is a very interesting book about sexual statistics. It identifies that American Indians have the longest average penis and Polish men have the biggest average diameter. By the way, my name is Jill. What's yours?" He coolly replies, "Tonto Kawalski, nice to meet you."

Persistence might pay

One night, as a couple lay down for bed, the husband gently taps his wife on the shoulder and starts rubbing her arm. The wife turns over and says: "I'm sorry honey, I've got a gynaecologist appointment tomorrow and I want to stay fresh." The husband, rejected, turns over and tries to sleep. A few minutes later, he rolls back over and taps his wife again. This time he whispers in her ear: "Do you have a dentist appointment tomorrow too?"

The pickle slicer

Bill worked in a pickle factory. He had been employed there for a number of years when he came home one day to confess to his wife that he had a terrible compulsion. He had an urge to stick his penis into the pickle slicer. His wife suggested that he should see a sex therapist to talk about it, but Bill indicated that he'd be too embarrassed. He vowed to overcome the compulsion on his own. One day a few weeks later, Bill came home absolutely ashen. His wife could see at once that something was seriously wrong. "What's wrong, Bill?" she asked. "Do you remember that I told you how I had this tremendous urge to put my penis into the pickle slicer?" "Oh, Bill, you didn't." "Yes, I did." "My God, Bill, what happened?" "I got fired." "No, Bill. I mean, what happened with the pickle slicer?" "Oh…she got fired too."

Whoops

A man was visiting his wife in hospital where she has been in a coma for several years. On this visit he decides to rub her left breast instead of just talking to her. On doing this she lets out a sigh. The man runs out and tells the doctor who says this is a good sign and suggests he should try rubbing her right breast to see if there is any reaction. The man goes in and rubs her right breast and this brings a moan. From this, the doctor suggests that the man should go in and try oral sex, saying he will wait outside as it is a personal act and he doesn't want the man to be embarrassed. The man goes in then comes out about five minutes later, white as a sheet and tells the doctor his wife is dead. The doctor asks what happened to which the man replies: "She choked."

Opportunist

A guy walks into a bar with a pet alligator by his side. He puts the alligator up on the bar. He turns to the astonished patrons. "I'll make you a deal. I'll open this alligator's mouth and place my genitals inside. Then the gator will close his mouth for one minute. He'll then open his mouth and I'll remove my unit unscathed. In return for witnessing this spectacle, each of you will buy me a drink." The crowd murmured their approval. The man stood up on the bar, dropped his trousers, and placed his privates in the alligator's open mouth. The gator closed his mouth as the crowd gasped. After a minute, the man grabbed a beer bottle and rapped the alligator hard on the top of its head. The gator opened his mouth and the man removed his genitals unscathed as promised. The crowd cheered and the first of his free drinks were delivered. The man stood up again and made another offer. "I'll pay anyone $100 who's willing to give it a try". A hush fell over the crowd. After a while, a hand went up in the back of the bar. A woman timidly spoke up. "I'll try, but you have to promise not to hit me on the head with the beer bottle".

Check that hearing

A small white guy goes into an elevator, when he gets in he notices a huge black dude standing next to him. The big black dude looks down upon the small white guy and says: "7 foot tall, 350 pounds, 20 inch dick, 3 pound left ball, 3 pound right ball, Turner Brown" The small white guy faints!! The big black dude picks up the small white guy and brings him to, slapping his face and shaking him and asks the small white guy. "What's wrong?" The small white guy says; "Excuse me but what did you say?" The big black dude looks down and says "7 foot tall, 350 pounds, 20 inch dick, 3 pound left ball, 3 pound right ball, my name is Turner Brown." The small white guy says, "Thank god, I thought you said 'Turn around. '"

The L0VE Dress

A woman stopped by unannounced at her recently married son's house. She rang the doorbell and walked in. She was shocked to see her daughter-in-law lying on the couch, totally naked. soft music was playing, and the aroma of perfume filled the room.

"What are you doing?" she asked. "I'm waiting for my husband to come home from work," the daughter-in-law answered." But you're naked!" the mother-in-law exclaimed." This is my L0VE dress," the daughter-in-law explained."L0VE dress? But you're naked!" "My husband L0VEs me to wear this dress," she explained.

"It excites him to no end. Every time he sees me in this dress, he instantly becomes romantic and ravages me for hours on end. He can't get enough of me."

The mother-in-law left. When she got home, she undressed, showered, put on her best perfume, dimmed the lights, put on a romantic CD, and laid on the couch waiting for her husband to arrive. Finally, her husband came home. He walked in and saw her laying there so provocatively "What are you doing?" he asked.

"This is my L0VE dress," she whispered, sensually.

"Needs ironing," he said. "What's for dinner?"

Essex Girls

A train hits a busload of Essex Schoolgirls and they all perish. They are all in heaven trying to enter the pearly gates past St. Peter. St Peter asks the first girl (from Southend), "Karen, have you ever had any contact with a mans thing?" She giggles and shyly replies, "Well I once touched the head of one with the tip of my finger" St. Peter says, "OK, dip the tip of your finger in The Holy Water and pass through the gate." St. Peter asks the next girl (from Chelmsford) the same question, "Joanne have you ever had any contact with a mans thing?" The girl is a little reluctant but replies "Well once I fondled and stroked one." St. Peter says, "OK, dip your whole hand in The Holy Water and pass through the gate." All of a sudden there is a lot of commotion in the line of girls, and the girl from Basildon is pushing her way to the front of the line. When she reaches the front of the line St. Peter says

"Tracy! What seems to be the rush?" The girl replies..
"If I'm going to have to gargle that Holy water…I want to do it before

Sharon sticks her arse in it!!"

The revelation

An old cowboy sat down at the bar and ordered a drink. As he sat sipping his whiskey, a young woman sat down next to him. She turned to the cowboy and asked, "Are you a real cowboy?"

He replied, "Well, I've spent my whole life on the ranch, herding horses, mending fences, and branding cattle, so I guess I am."

She said, "I'm a lesbian.. I spend my whole day thinking about women. As soon as I get up in the morning, I think about women; when I shower I think

about women. When I watch TV I think about women. I even think about women when I eat. It seems that everything makes me think of women." The two sat sipping in silence.

A little while later, a man sat down on the other side of the old cowboy and asked, "Are you a real cowboy?"

The cowboy replied, "I always thought I was, but I just found out I'm a lesbian.

Cowboys

Two cowboys from Arizona walk into a roadhouse to wash the trail dust from their throats. They stand at the bar, drinking their beers and talking quietly about cattle prices. This is good!!!!!!!!

Suddenly a woman at a table behind them, who had been eating a sandwich, begins to cough. After a minute or so it becomes apparent that she is in real distress, and the cowboys turn to look at her.

"Kin ya swaller?" asks one of the cowboys. The woman signals No, desperately shaking her head. Kin ya breathe?" asks the other.

The woman, beginning to turn a bit blue, shakes her head "No" again.

The first cowboy walks over to her, lifts up the back of her skirt, yanks down her pants, and slowly runs his tongue up and down the woman's butt crack. This shocks the woman to a violent spasm, the obstruction flies out of her mouth, and she begins to breathe again. The cowboy slowly walks back over to the bar and proudly takes a drink of his beer. His partner says in admiration, "Ya know, I'd heard of that there Hind Lick Manoeuvre, but I ain't never seen nobody do it."

Keith

A man walks up to a woman in his office each day, stands very close to her, draws in a large breath of air and tells her that her hair smells nice.

After a week of this, she can't stand it any longer, and goes to Human Resources.

Without identifying the guy, she tells them what the co-worker does, and that she wants to file a sexual harassment suit against him.

The HR supervisor is puzzled by this approach, and asks, "What's sexually threatening about a co-worker telling you your hair smells nice?"

The woman replies, "It's Keith, the midget"

The Gift

A young man wanted to buy a gift for his girlfriend's birthday, they had not been together very long so he thought long and hard before remembering that on their last date she had complained that her hands were cold. So he decided on a pair of gloves, not too personal at this stage of their relationship, but thoughtful nonetheless.

Accompanied by his girlfriend's sister he went to Harrods and bought a stylish pair of dainty white gloves. At the same time the sister bought a pair of knickers for herself and they both asked for them to be gift-wrapped. Unfortunately the shop assistant mixed the items up and the guy left with the gift-wrapped panties.

The boyfriend, obviously none the wiser, decided to deliver his present in person. When he arrived at his girlfriend's house she wasn't in. So instead he left the following, thoughtful note along with the present at her front door.

"I hope you like your present, I chose these because I noticed that you are not in the habit of wearing any when we go out in the evening. Had it not been for your sister I would have chosen some long ones with white buttons, but she wears short ones and they are easier to pull off. These are a delicate shade and the shop assistant showed me the pair she had been wearing for the past three weeks and they are hardly soiled at all. I had her try on yours and although a little tight they looked really smart. She told me that the material keeps her ring clean and shiny and in fact she hadn't had to wash it since wearing them. I wish you had been here so that I could have put them on for you as no doubt many hands will touch them before I have the chance to see you again. When you take them off, remember to blow into them, as they will be a little damp from wearing. Just think how many times I will be holding them in my hand over the coming year; I hope you will wear them for me on Friday night.

PS. The latest style is to wear them folded down with a little fur showing.

Great boss

Hung Chow calls his boss and says: "Hey, boss I not come work today, really sick. I got headache, stomach ache and my legs hurt, I not come work."

The boss says: "You know Hung Chow I really need you today. When I feel like this I go to my wife and tell her to give me sex. That makes me feel better and I can go to work. You should try that."

Two hours later Hung Chow calls again: "Boss, I do what you say and feel great, I be at work soon. You got nice house."

Why Fishing is better than sex:

1. You don't have to hide your Fishing magazines.

2. It's perfectly acceptable to pay a professional to Fish with you once in a while.

3. The Ten Commandments don't say anything about Fishing.

4. If your partner takes pictures or videotapes of you Fishing in your Whaler, you don't have to worry about them showing up on the Internet if you become famous.

5. Your Fishing partner doesn't get upset about people you fished with long ago.

6. It's perfectly respectable to Fish with a total stranger.

7. When you see a really good Fisher person, you don't have feel guilty about imagining the two of you Fishing in a Whaler together.

8. If your regular Fishing partner isn't available, he/she won't object if you Fish with someone else.

9. Nobody will ever tell you that you will go blind if you Fish by yourself.

10. When dealing with a Fishing pro, you never have to wonder if they are really an undercover cop.

11. You can have a Fishing calendar on your wall at the office, tell Fishing jokes, and invite co-workers to Fish with you without getting sued for harassment.

12. There are no Fishing-transmitted diseases.

13. If you want to watch Fishing on television, you don't have to subscribe to the Playboy channel.

14. Nobody expects you to Fish with the same partner for the rest of your life.

15. Nobody expects you to give up Fishing if your partner loses interest in it.

16. Your Fishing partner will never say, "Not again? We just fished last week! Is Fishing all you ever think about?"

Affairs

The First Affair

There was a middle-age couple that had two stunningly beautiful teen-age daughters. The couple decided to try one last time for the son they always wanted. After months of trying, the wife became pregnant and, sure enough, delivered a healthy baby boy nine months later. The joyful father rushed to the nursery to see his new son. He took one look and was horrified to find the ugliest child he had ever seen. He went to his wife and said that there was no way that he could be the father of the child.

"Look at the two beautiful daughters I fathered," he cried. Then he gave her a stern look and asked, "Have you been fooling around on me?" The wife smiled sweetly and said, "Not this time."

The Second Affair

A mortician was working late one night. It was his job to examine the dead bodies before they were sent off to be buried or cremated. As he examined the body of Mr. Schwartz, he made an amazing discovery:

Schwartz had the longest private part he had ever seen! "I'm sorry, Mr Schwartz," said the mortician, "but I can't send you off to be cremated with a tremendously huge private part like this. It has to be saved for posterity." And with that the coroner used his tools to remove the dead man's privates.

The coroner stuffed his prize into a briefcase and took it home. The first person he showed was his wife. "I have something to show you that you won't believe," he said, opening his briefcase. "Oh, my God!" she screamed. "Schwartz is dead!"

The Third Affair

A woman was in bed with her lover when she heard her husband opening the front door. "Hurry!" she said. "Stand in the corner!" She quickly rubbed baby oil all over him and then she dusted him with talcum powder. "Don't move until I tell you to," she whispered. "Just pretend you're a statue." "What's this, honey?" the husband inquired as he entered the room. "Oh, it's just a statue," she replied nonchalantly. "The Smiths bought one for their bedroom. I liked it so much, I got one for us, too." No more was said about the statue, not even later that night when they went to sleep.

Around 2 a.m., the husband got out of bed, went to the kitchen and returned a while later with a sandwich and a glass of milk. "Here," he said to the statue, "eat something. I stood like an idiot at the Smiths' for three days, and nobody offered me as much as a glass of water."

The Fourth Affair

A man walks into a bar one night. He goes up to the bartender and asks for a beer. "Certainly, sir," replies the bartender. "That'll be 1 cent. "ONE CENT!" exclaims the customer. The barman replies, "Yes." So the guy glances over the menu and asks, "Could I have a nice juicy T-bone steak with chips, peas and a fried egg?" "Certainly, sir," replies the bartender, "but all that comes to real money." "How much money?"

inquires the guy. "Four cents, "the bartender replies. "FOUR cents!" exclaims the guy. "Where's the guy who owns this place?"

The bartender replies, "Upstairs with my wife." The guy asks, "What's he doing with your wife?" The bartender replies, "Same as I'm doing to his business."

The Fifth Affair

Jake was dying. His wife, Becky, was maintaining a candlelight vigil by his side. She held his fragile hand, tears running down her face.

Her praying roused him from his slumber. He looked up and his pale lips began to move slightly, "My darling Becky," he whispered. "Hush, my love," she said. "Rest. Shhh, don't talk." He was insistent. "Becky," he said in his tired voice, "I have something I must confess to you." "There's nothing to confess," replied the weeping Becky. "Everything's all right. Go to sleep."

"No, no, I must die in peace, Becky. I slept with your sister, your best friend, her best friend and your mother!" "I know," Becky whispered softly. "That's why I poisoned you."

Parrots

An old man was sitting on a bench, when a young man walked up and sat down next to him. The young man had spiked hair in all different colours red, green yellow orange and blue. The old man just stared. Every time the young man looked, the old man was staring.

The young man finally said sarcastically....." What's the matter old timer, never done anything wild in your life"

Without batting an eye, the old man replied," Got drunk once and had sex with a parrot ... I was just wondering if you were my son"

Death Grip

One morning while making breakfast, a man walked up to his wife and pinched her on the butt and said, "If you firmed this up, we could get rid of your control top pantyhose." While this was on the edge of intolerable, she kept silent. The next morning, the man woke his wife with a pinch on each of her breasts and said, "You know, if you firmed these up, we could get rid of your bra." This was beyond a silent response, so she rolled over and grabbed him by his penis. With a death grip in place, she said, "You know, if you firmed this up, we could get rid of the gardener, the postman, the poolman, and your brother."

Sexual Calorie Counter

It has been known for many years that sex is good exercise, but until recently nobody had made a scientific study of the calorific expenditure of different sexual activities. Now, after original and proprietary research, they are proud to present the results.

REMOVING HER CLOTHES:
With her consent......................12 calories
Without her consent...................187 calories

OPENING HER BRA:
With both hands……………………8 calories
With one hand……………………12 calories
With your teeth ……………………85 calories

PUTTING ON A CONDOM:
With an erection……………………6 calories
Without an erection…………………315 calories

PRELIMINARIES:
Trying to find the clitoris……………8 calories
Trying to find the G spot……………92 calories

POSITIONS:
Missionary……………………………52 calories
69 lying down………………………78 calories
69 standing up………………………112 calories
Wheelbarrow…………………………216 calories
Her on top……………………………524 calories
Doggy style…………………………726 calories
Donkey punch………………………912 calories

ORGASMIC:
Real……………………………………112 calories
False……………………………………315 calories

POST ORGASM:
Lying in bed hugging………………18 calories
Getting up immediately……………36 calories
Explaining why you got out of bed immediately
.   816 calories

GETTING A SECOND ERECTION:
If you are:
20-29 years old……………………36 calories
30-39 years……………………….80 calories
40-49 years……………………….1124 calories
50-59 years……………………….1972 calories
60-69 years……………………….2916 calories
70 and over……………Results are still pending

GETTING DRESSED AFTERWARDS:
Calmly…………………………….32 calories
In a hurry…………………………98 calories
With her father knocking at the door.1218 calories
With your spouse knocking at the door 5521 calories

The Penis' Request

The Penis hereby requests a raise in salary for the following

reasons:
a.. I do physical labour
b.. I work at great depths
c.. I plunge head first into everything I do
d.. I do not get weekends or public holidays off
e.. I work in a damp environment
f.. I don't get paid overtime
g.. I work in a dark workplace that has poor ventilation
h.. I work in high temperatures
i.. My work exposes me to contagious diseases

Dear Penis,

After assessing your request, and considering the arguments you have raised, the administration rejects your request for the following reasons:

a. You do not work 8 hours straight

b. You fall asleep on the job after brief work period's

c. You do not always follow the orders of the management team

d. You do not stay in your designated area and are often seen visiting other locations

e. You do not take initiative - you need to be pressured and stimulated in order to start working

f. You leave the workplace rather messy at the end of your shift

g. You don't always observe necessary safety regulations, such as wearing the correct protective clothing

h. You will retire well before you are 65

i. You are unable to work double shifts

j. You sometimes leave your designated work area before you have completed the days work

k. And if that were not all, you have been seen constantly entering and exiting the workplace carrying two suspicious-looking bags.

Sincerely,

The Management

The Chemists

A man went into a chemist and asked to talk to a male pharmacist.

The woman he was talking to said that she was the pharmacist and that she and her sister owned the store, so there were no males employed there. She then asked if there was something that she could help the gentleman with.

The man said that it was something that he would be much more comfortable discussing with a male pharmacist.

"Fear not", the female pharmacist assured him, "because she was a professional and whatever it was that he needed to discuss, he could be confident that she would treat him with the highest level of professionalism".

The man agreed and began by saying, "This is tough for me to discuss, but I have a permanent erection. It causes me a lot of problems and severe embarrassment. So I was wondering what you could give me for it?

The pharmacist said, "Just a minute, I'll go talk to my sister."

When she returned, she said, "We discussed it at length and the absolute best we can do is 1/3 ownership in the store, a company car, plus £6000 a month living expenses."

Quick thinking

A man boards an aeroplane and takes his seat. As he settles in, he glances up and sees a most beautiful woman boarding the 'plane.

He soon realizes she is heading straight towards his seat. A wave of nervous anticipation washes over him. Lo and behold, she takes the seat right beside his. Eager to strike up a conversation, he blurts out, "Business trip or vacation?".

"Nymphomaniac Convention in London," she states.

Whoa!!! He swallows hard and is instantly crazed with excitement.

Here's the most gorgeous woman he has ever seen, sitting RIGHT next to him and she's going to a meeting of nymphomaniacs! Struggling to maintain his outward cool, he calmly asks, "What's your business role at this convention?" "Lecturer", she says. "I use my experiences to debunk some of the popular myths about sexuality."

"Really," he says, swallowing hard, "what myths are those?"

"Well," she explains, "one popular myth is that African American men are the most well-endowed when, in fact, it is the Native American Indian who is most likely to possess that trait. Another popular myth is that French men are the best lovers, when actually it is men of Greek descent."

Suddenly, the woman becomes very embarrassed and blushes. "I'm sorry," she says, "I shouldn't be discussing this with you, I don't even know your name!"

"Tonto," the man says, as he extends his hand. "Tonto Papadopoulos."

What a gent

One night a guy takes his girlfriend home. As they are about to kiss each other goodnight at the front door, the guy starts feeling a little horny. With an air of confidence, he leans with his hand against the wall and smiling, he says to her.

"Honey, would you give me a blow job?"

Horrified, she replies, "Are you mad? My parents will see us!"

"Oh come on! Who's gonna see us at this hour?"
"No, please. Can you imagine if we get caught?"
"Oh come on! There's nobody around, they're all sleeping!"

"No way. It's just too risky!"
"Oh please, please, I love you so much!"
"No, no and no" "I love you too, but I just can't!"
"Oh yes you can. Please?"
"No, no. I just can't"
"I'm begging you …"

Out of the blue, the light on the stairs goes on, and the girl's sister shows up in her pyjamas, hair dishevelled, and in a sleepy voice she says,

"Dad says to go ahead and give him a blow job, or I can do it. Or if need be, Mum says she can come down herself and do it. But for god sake, tell him to take his hand off the intercom."

The seven dwarfs

The Seven Dwarfs go to the Vatican and, because they have requested an audience, and as they are The Seven Dwarfs, they are ushered in to see the Pope. Dopey leads the pack.

"Dopey, my son," says the Pope, "what can I do for you?"

Dopey asks, "Excuse me, Your Holiness, but are there any dwarf nuns in Rome?"

The Pope wrinkles his brow at the odd question, thinks for a moment, and answers, "No, Dopey, there are no dwarf nuns in Rome."

In the background a few of the dwarfs start giggling. Dopey turns around and gives them a glare, silencing them.

Dopey turns back, "Your Worship, are there any dwarf nuns in all of Europe?"

The Pope, puzzled now, again thinks for a moment and then answers, "Dopey, there are no dwarf nuns in Europe."

This time, all of the other dwarfs burst into laughter. Once again, Dopey turns around and silences them with an angry glare.

Dopey turns back and says, "Your extreme holiness! Are there ANY dwarf nuns anywhere in the world?"

After consulting with his advisors, the Pope responds, "I'm sorry my son, there're no dwarf nuns anywhere in the world."

The other dwarfs collapse in a heap, rolling, laughing and pounding the floor, tears streaming down their cheeks as they begin chanting......

"Dopey shagged a penguin! .....Dopey shagged a penguin!......"

The kinds of sex

The first kind of sex is Smurf Sex.

This kind of sex happens when you first meet someone and you both have sex until you are blue in the face.

The second kind of sex is Kitchen Sex.

This is when you have been with your partner for a short time and you're so horny you will have sex anywhere, even in the kitchen.

The third kind of sex is Bedroom Sex.

This is when you have been with your partner for a long time. Your sex has gotten routine and you usually have sex in your bedroom.

The fourth kind of sex is Hallway Sex.

This is when you have been with your partner for too long. When you pass each other in the hallway you both say "Fuck You."

The fifth kind of sex is Courtroom Sex.

This is when you cannot stand each other any more. She takes you to court and screws you in front of everyone.

Husband wanted

A midwife asked a young lady in the maternity ward just prior to labour if she would like her husband to be present at the birth.

"I'm afraid I don't have a husband," she replied.

"O.K., do you have a boyfriend?" asked the Midwife.

"No, no boyfriend either."

"Do you have a partner then?"

"No, I'm unattached, I'll be having the baby on my own."

After the birth, the midwife again spoke to the young woman.

"You have a healthy bouncing baby girl, but I must let you know before you see her that the baby is black."

"Well," replied the girl. "I was very down on my luck, with no money and nowhere to live, and so I accepted a job in a porno movie. The lead man was black."

"Oh, I'm very sorry," said the midwife, that's really none of my business, and I'm sorry that I have to ask you these awkward questions, but I must also tell you that the baby has blonde hair."

"Well, yes," the girl again replied. "You see, I desperately needed the money and there was this Swedish guy also involved in the movie.......What else could I do?"

"Oh, I'm so sorry," the midwife repeated. "That's really none of my business either and I hate to pry further, but your baby has slanted eyes." "Well, yes," continued the girl. "I was incredibly hard up and there was a little Chinese man also in the movie. I really had no choice

At this, the midwife again apologised, collected the baby, and presented her to the girl, who immediately proceeded to give the baby a slap on the bum.

The baby started crying and the mother exclaimed "Well, thank God for that!" "What do you mean?" said the midwife, shocked.

"Well," said the girl, extremely relieved, "I had this horrible feeling it was going to bark!"

Voodoo Penis

A businessman was getting ready to go on a long business trip. He knew his wife was a flirtatious sort with an extremely healthy sex drive, so he thought he'd buy her a little something to keep her occupied while he was gone.

He went to a store that sold sex toys and started to look around. He thought about a life-sized sex doll, but that was too close to another man for him. He was browsing through the dildo's, looking for something special to please his wife, and started talking to the old man behind the counter. He explained his situation.

"Well, I don't really know of anything that will do the trick. We have vibrating dildos, special attachments, and so on, but I don't know of thing that will keep her occupied for weeks, except..." and he stopped.

"Except what?" the man asked.

"Nothing, nothing."

"C'mon, tell me! I need something!"

"Well, sir, I don't usually mention this, but there is The Voodoo penis."

"So what's up with this Voodoo Penis?" he asked.

The old man reached under the counter, and pulled out a very old wooden box, carved with strange symbols and erotic images. He opened it, and there laid an ordinary-looking dildo.

The businessman laughed, and said "Big damn deal. It looks like every other dildo in this shop!"

The old man replied, "But you haven't seen what it'll do yet." He pointed to a door and said "Voodoo Penis, the door." The Voodoo Penis miraculously rose out of its box, darted over to the door, and started pounding the keyhole. The whole door shook wildly with the vibrations, so much so that a crack began to form down the middle. Before the door split, the old man said "Voodoo Penis, return to box!" The Voodoo Penis stopped, levitated back to the box and lay there quiescent once more.

"I'll take it!" said the businessman. The old man resisted, saying it wasn't for sale, but finally surrendered to $738 in cash and an imitation Rolex. The guy took it home to his wife, told her it was a special dildo and that to use it, all she had to do was say "Voodoo Penis, my crotch." He left for his trip satisfied that things would be fine while he was gone. After he'd been gone a few days, his wife was unbearably horny. She thought of several people who would willingly satisfy her, but then she remembered the Voodoo Penis. She undressed, opened the box and said, "Voodoo Penis, my crotch!" The Voodoo Penis shot to her crotch and started pumping. It was absolutely incredible, like nothing she'd ever experienced before. After three mind-shattering orgasms, she became very exhausted and decided she'd had enough. She tried to pull it out, but it was stuck in her, still thrusting. She tried and tried to get it out, but nothing worked. Her husband had forgotten to tell her how to shut it off.

Worried, she decided to go to the hospital to see if they could help. She put her clothes on, got in the car and started to drive, quivering with every thrust of the dildo. On the way, another incredible intense orgasm made her swerve all over the road. A police officer saw this and immediately pulled her over. He asked for her license, and then asked how much she'd had to drink. Gasping and twitching, she explained, "I haven't had anything to drink, officer. You see, I've got this Voodoo Penis thing stuck in my crotch and it won't stop screwing me!" The officer looked at her for a second, shook his head and in an arrogant voice replied, "Yeah, right… Voodoo Penis, my ass!"

James Bond

James Bond walks into a bar and takes a seat next to very attractive woman. He gives her a quick glance, then casually looks at his watch for a moment. The women notices this and asks, "Is your date running late?" "No", he replies, "Q's just given me this state-of-the-art watch and I was just testing it." The intrigued woman says, "A state-of-the-art watch? What's so Special about it?"

Bond explains, "It uses alpha waves to talk to me telepathically the lady says, what's it telling you now?" "Well, it says you're not wearing any knickers…." The woman giggles and replies, "Well it must be broken because I am wearing knickers!" Bond tuts, taps his watch and says, "Damn thing's an hour fast."

After the wedding

A Mother had 3 virgin daughters. They were all getting married within a short time period. Because Mum was a bit worried about how their sex life would get started, she made them all promise to send a postcard from the honeymoon with a few words on how marital sex felt.

The first girl sent a card from Cape Town two days after the wedding. The card said nothing but "Nescafe". Mum was puzzled at first, but then went the kitchen and got out the Nescafe jar. It said: "Good till the last drop." Mum blushed, but was pleased for her daughter.

The second girl sent the card from Sydney a week after the wedding, and the card read: "Benson & Hedges". Mum now knew to go straight to her husband's cigarettes, and she read from the Benson & Hedges pack: "Extra Long. King Size". She was again slightly embarrassed but still happy for her daughter.

The third girl left for her honeymoon in the Caribbean. Mum waited for a week, nothing. Another week went by and still nothing. Then after a whole month, a card finally arrived. Written on it with shaky handwriting were the words "British Airways". Mum took out her latest Harper's Bazaar magazine, flipped through the pages fearing the worst, and finally found the ad for British Airways. The ad said: "Three times a day, seven days a week, both ways." Mom fainted…..

Live on the radio

This story occurred on Australian radio. One of the FM stations has a competition where they ring someone up, ask them three personal questions, ring their spouse or partner, ask them the same three questions, if the answers are the same, the couple win a holiday to Bali. Last week the competition went like this:

Presenter: Gidday Brian, are you ready to play the game?

Brian: Yeah, sure.

Presenter: O.K., Question 1 - When was the last time you had sex?

Brian: Ohhh, maaaate. Ha Ha, well, about 8 o'clock this morning.

Presenter: And how long did it go for Brian?

Brian: Orrrrr …. about 10 minutes.

Presenter: 10 minutes? Good one. And where did you do it mate?

Brian: Ohhhh maaaaate, I can't say that.

Presenter: There's a holiday to Bali at stake here Brian!

Brian: O.K. … O.K. … On the kitchen table.

Presenter: (and others in the room - much laughter). Good one Brian,

Now is it O.K. for us to call your wife?

Brian: Yeah, alright.

Presenter: Hi Sharelle, how are you?

Sharelle: Hi. Good thanks.

Presenter: (Explains competition again) We've got Brian on the other line, say hello.

Sharelle: Hi Brian.

Brian: Hi Sharelle.

Presenter: Now Sharelle, we're going to ask you the same three questions we asked Brian and if you give the same answers, you win a trip for two to Bali.

Brian: Just tell the truth Honey.

Sharelle: O.K.

Presenter: Sharelle, when was the last time you had sex?

Sharelle: Oohhhh, noooooo. I can't say that on radio.

Brian: Sharelle, it doesn't matter. I've already told them.

Sharelle: O.K. ... About 8:00 this morning before Brian went to work.

Presenter: Good, nice start! Next question. How long did it go for Sharelle?

Sharelle: (giggling) About 12, maybe 15 minutes.

Co-Presenter: That's close enough ... Brian was just being a gentleman.

Presenter: O.K. Sharelle, final question. Where did you do it?

Sharelle: Oh no I can't say that. My mum could be listening. No way, no.

Presenter: There's a trip to Bali on the line here.

Brian: Sharelle, I've already told them so it doesn't matter anyway…just tell em.

Sharelle: Ohhhh …. alright …. Up the arse!

Radio Silence.

Advert.

Presenter: Sorry if anyone was offended before, we're going live here, and sometimes these things happen. We've given Brian and Sharelle the holiday.

Now we'll take a music break.

New neighbour

Joe leased an apartment and went to the lobby to put his name on his mailbox. While there, an attractive young lady came out of the apartment next to the mailboxes wearing a robe Joe smiled at the young woman and she started a conversation with him. As they talked, her robe slipped open, and it was obvious that she had nothing else on; Poor Joe broke out into a sweat trying to maintain eye contact.

After a few minutes, she placed her hand on his arm and said, "Let's go to my apartment, I hear someone coming." He followed her into her apartment, she closed the door and leaned against it, allowing her robe to fall off completely. Now nude, she purred at him, "What would you say is my best feature? Flustered and embarrassed, Joe finally squeaked, "It's got to be your ears!"

Astounded and a little hurt she asked, "My ears? Look at these breasts; they are full and 100% natural! I work out every day! My butt is firm and solid! Look at my skin no blemishes anywhere! How can you feel the best part of my body is my ears?" Clearing his throat, Joe stammered, "Outside, when you said you heard someone coming? That was me."

Vive La Difference

GIRL'S DIARY
FRIDAY 21st June 2002.

Saw John in the evening and he was acting really strangely. I went shopping in the afternoon with the girls and I did turn up a bit late so

I thought it might be that.

The bar was really crowded and loud so I suggested we go somewhere quieter to talk.

He was still very subdued and distracted so I suggested we go somewhere nice to eat.

All through dinner he just didn't seem himself; he hardly laughed, and didn't seem to be paying any attention to me or to what I was saying. I just knew that something was wrong.

He dropped me back home and I wondered if he was going to come in; he hesitated, but followed.

I asked him again if there was something the matter but he just half shook his head and turned the television on.

After about 10 minutes of silence, I said I was going upstairs to bed.

I put my arms around him and told him that I loved him deeply. He just gave a sigh, and a sad sort of smile.

He didn't follow me up, but later he did, and I was surprised when we made love.

He still seemed distant and a bit cold, and started to think that he was going to leave me, and that he had found someone else. I cried myself to sleep.

BOY'S DIARY
FRIDAY 21st June 2002.
England lost to Brazil 2-1. Got a shag though.

Prayers

A Girls Prayer

Lord

Before I lay me down to sleep,
I pray for a man, who's not a creep,
One who's handsome, smart and strong,
One who's willy's thick and long.
One who thinks before he speaks,
When promises to call, he won't wait weeks.

I pray that he is gainfully employed,
And when I spend his cash, wont be annoyed.
Pulls out my chair and opens my door,
Massages my back and begs to do more.

Oh! send me a man who will make love to my mind,
Knows just what to say, when I ask "How big's my behind?"
One who'll make love till my body's a twitchin,
In the hall, the loo, the garden and kitchen!

I pray that this man will love me no end,
And never attempts to shag my best friend.
And as I kneel and pray by my bed,
I look at the w**ker you sent me instead.

Amen.

A Boy's Prayer:

Lord
I pray for a lady with big tits
Amen

COMPILED BY ROY VEGA

The truth about men and women

THE TRUTH ABOUT "GIRLIES"

1. Properties

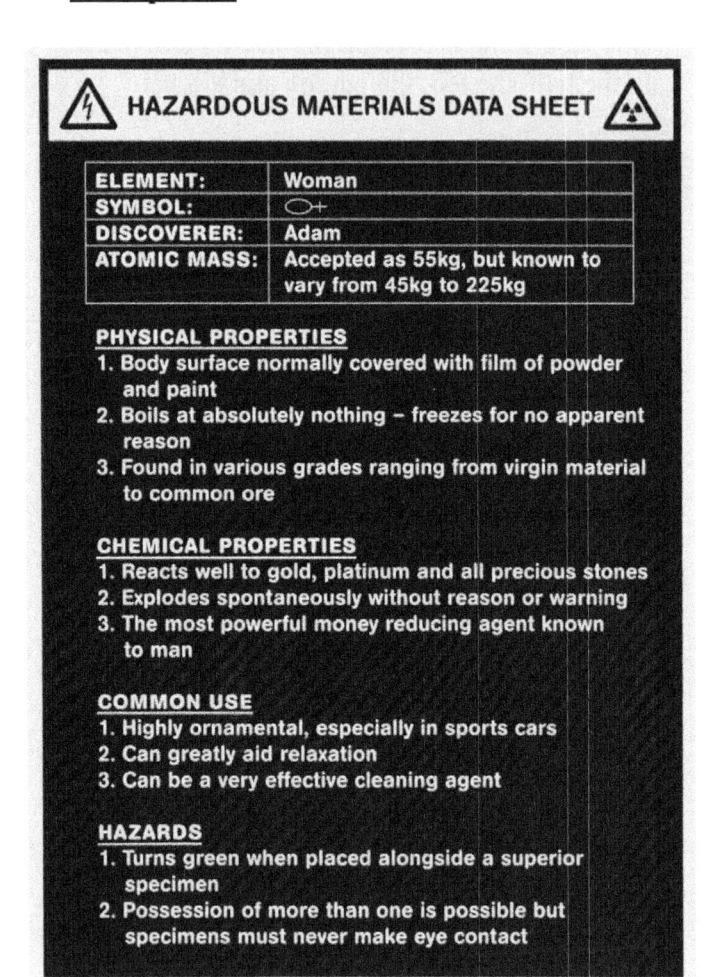

⚠ HAZARDOUS MATERIALS DATA SHEET ☢

ELEMENT:	Woman
SYMBOL:	♀
DISCOVERER:	Adam
ATOMIC MASS:	Accepted as 55kg, but known to vary from 45kg to 225kg

PHYSICAL PROPERTIES
1. Body surface normally covered with film of powder and paint
2. Boils at absolutely nothing – freezes for no apparent reason
3. Found in various grades ranging from virgin material to common ore

CHEMICAL PROPERTIES
1. Reacts well to gold, platinum and all precious stones
2. Explodes spontaneously without reason or warning
3. The most powerful money reducing agent known to man

COMMON USE
1. Highly ornamental, especially in sports cars
2. Can greatly aid relaxation
3. Can be a very effective cleaning agent

HAZARDS
1. Turns green when placed alongside a superior specimen
2. Possession of more than one is possible but specimens must never make eye contact

2. Shopping Mission

Mission: Go to Gap, Buy a Pair of Pants

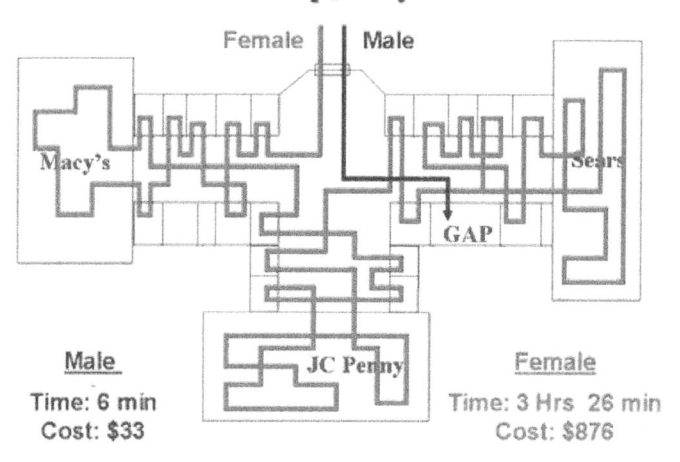

Female | Male

Macy's
Sears
GAP
JC Penny

Male
Time: 6 min
Cost: $33

Female
Time: 3 Hrs 26 min
Cost: $876

3. Simple fact of life

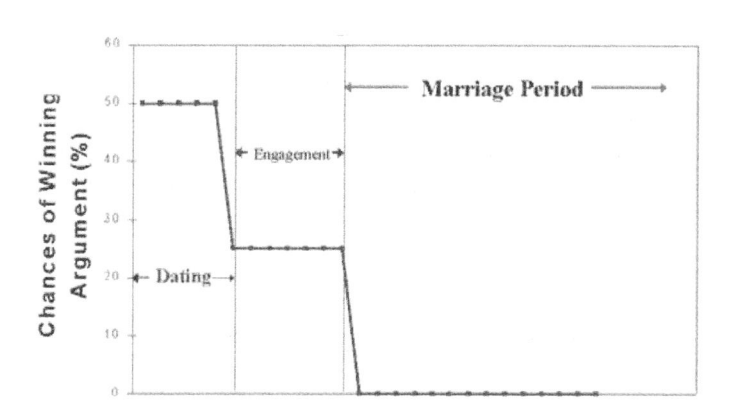

Chances of Winning Argument (%)

← Dating →
← Engagement →
← Marriage Period →

4. Control

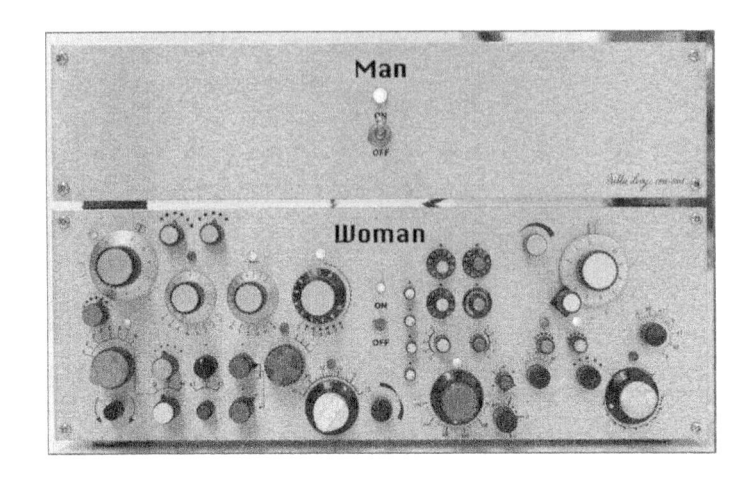

5. But ....When It Comes To Common Sense................

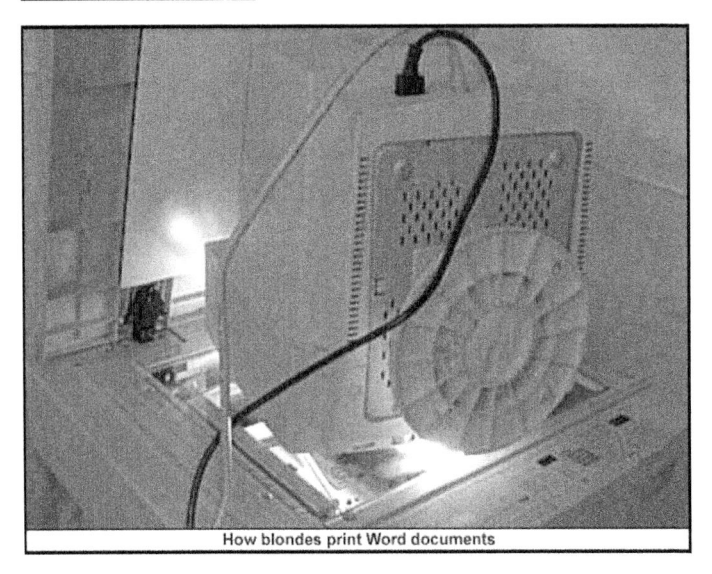

How blondes print Word documents

Toilet humour

15 Easy Steps to use the smallest room like a lady

1. Under no circumstances use any other toilet than your own, regardless of any stomach pain may be caused whilst waiting to get home.
2. With the toilet-brush, clean any residue left on the pan by your boyfriend/husband. Also wipe his pubic hair off the seat with some toilet paper.
3. Flush the toilet before starting. Then wash your hands.
4. Line the toilet seat with toilet paper (as other people may have sat on the toilet since it was last bleached).
5. Stuff toilet paper inside the pan to prevent splash-back.
6. Pull panties down and sit. Some women may still prefer to squat over the seat as opposed to taking the risk of touching it with bare flesh.
7. Release solids, but strain to avoid making any sounds.
8. Rise and quickly flush before direct eye-contact is made with any faeces.
9. Take a length of toilet paper and fold it several times to positively guarantee that no residue will touch bare skin (about five or six applications per roll).
10. Wipe once and throw paper into the pan. Do not look at the paper.

11. Repeat steps 9 and 10 at least thirty times. It may be necessary to yell for your boyfriend/husband to find some more rolls to pass through the door while promising not to open his eyes or pass any comments. It is traditional to do this while he is trying to watch sport.
12. Flush the toilet and replace the lid.
13. Wash hands at least three times with disinfectant soap.
14. Open all windows and spray approximately half-a-can of air freshener.
15. Pick up all reading material left behind by your boyfriend/husband and leave bathroom, closing the door firmly behind you.

15 Easy Steps to Poo like a Man:

1. Select reading material
2. Tell everyone along the way, "Just going for a dump, okay?" Always tell girlfriend/wife, especially when she has visitors.
3. Pull pants and trousers around ankles, then sit down.
4. Adjust penis and testicles to hang comfortably without touching the toilet rim.
5. Open reading material and relax.
6. Whilst waiting, it is traditional to audibly fart.
7. Sigh loudly as the first one bullets out. It is quite normal to experience a cold jet of water rocket up your anus as a result of the first bomb. This is to be endured if you want to be a real man.

8. Remain sitting and reading until pins-and-needles set in to your legs and buttocks.
9. Rise and look at the poo. Make mental notes of any irregularities to report to friends and girlfriend/wife, e.g. colour, consistency, any visible traces of peanuts, etc. You must tell people about it.
10. Take long length of paper and wipe anus. You must look at the paper before throwing it into the pan.
11. Repeat step 10 until there is no longer any evidence of faeces on the paper.
12. Flush. If there is any residue left on the pan, under no circumstances attempt to clean it off. In due course, it will come away by itself. Or, when your girlfriend/wife next uses the loo.
13. Leave the seat up. Leave the reading material on the floor (you can use it again later).
14. Wash your hands once.
15. Vacate the bathroom, leaving the door open. It is important to a man's self-esteem that other people smell his produce.

Amateur Psychiatry

The logical scientist

Two builders (Chris and James) are seated either side of a table in a rough pub when a well-dressed man enters, orders a beer and sits on a stool at the bar.

The two builders start to speculate about the occupation of the suit…

Chris: - I reckon he's an accountant.

James: - No way - he's a stockbroker.

Chris: - He ain't no stockbroker! A stockbroker wouldn't come in here!

The argument repeats itself for some time until the volume of beer gets the better of Chris and he makes for the toilet. On entering the toilet he sees that the suit is standing at a urinal. Curiosity and the several beers get the better of the builder…

Chris: - Scuse me…. no offence meant, but me and me mate were wondering what you do for a living?

Suit: - No offence taken! I'm a Logical Scientist by profession!

Chris: - Oh! What's that then?

Suit: - I'll try to explain by example …Do you have a goldfish at home?

Chris: - Er … mmm … well yeah, I do as it happens!

Suit: - Well, it's logical to follow that you keep it in a bowl or in a pond. Which is it?

Chris: - It's in a pond!

Suit: - Well then it's reasonable to suppose that you have a large garden then?

Chris: - As it happens, yes I have got a big garden!

Suit: - Well then it's logical to assume that in this town if you have a large garden then you have a large house?

Chris: - As it happens I've got a five bedroom house… built it myself!

Suit: - Well given that you've built a five bedroom house it is logical to assume that you haven't built it just for yourself and that you are quite probably married?

Chris: - Yes I am married, I live with my wife and three children!

Suit: - Well then it is logical to assume that you are sexually active with your wife on a regular basis?

Chris: - Yep! Four nights a week!

Suit: - Well then it is logical to suggest that you do not masturbate very often?

Chris: - Me? Never

Suit: - Well there you are! That's logical science at work!

Chris: - How's that then?

Suit: - Well from finding out that you had a goldfish, I've told you about your sex life!

Chris: - I see! That's pretty impressive... thanks mate!

Both leave the toilet and Chris returns to his mate.

James: - I see the suit was in there. Did you ask him what he does?

Chris: - Yep! He's a logical scientist!

James: - What's that then?

Chris: - I'll try and explain. Do you have a goldfish?

James: - Nope

Chris: - Well then, you're a wanker.

Pets

At the vets

A woman brought a very limp parrot into a veterinary surgery. As she laid her pet on the table, the vet pulled out his stethoscope and listened to the bird's chest. After a moment or two, the vet shook his head sadly and said, "I'm so sorry, Polly has passed away."

The distressed owner wailed, "Are you sure? I mean you haven't done any testing on him or anything. He might just be in a coma or something."

The vet rolled his eyes, shrugged, turned and left the zoom, returning a few moments later with a beautiful black Labrador. As the bird's owner looked on in amazement, the dog stood on his hind legs, put his front paws on the examination table and sniffed the dead parrot from top to bottom.

He then looked at the vet with sad eyes and shook his head.

The vet fussed the dog and took it out, but returned a few moments later with a cat. The cat jumped up and also sniffed delicately at the ex-bird. The cat sat back, shook its head, meowed and ran out of the room.

The vet looked at the woman and said, "I'm sorry, but like I said, your parrot is most definitely 100% certifiably ….. dead." He then turned to his computer terminal, hit a few keys and produced a bill which he handed to the woman. The parrot's owner, still in shock, took the bill.

"£150!, she cried, £150 just to tell me my bird is dead.!!"

The vet shrugged. "If you'd taken my word for it the bill would only have been £20, but what with the Lab report and the cat scan……"

What an octopus

A guy walks into a bar with an octopus. He sits the octopus down on a stool and tells everyone in the bar that this is a very talented octopus. He can play any instrument in the world. He hears everyone in the crowd laughing at him …so he says he will wager $50 to anyone who has an instrument that the octopus can't play.

A guy walks up with a guitar and sits it beside the octopus. The octopus starts playing better than Jimi Hendrix. So the man pays his $50.

Another guy walks up with a trumpet; the octopus plays the trumpet better than Dizzy Gillespie. So the man pays his $50.

A third guy walks up with bagpipes. He sits them down and the octopus fumbles with it for a minute and sets it down with a confused look. "Ha!" the man says, "can't you play it?" The octopus looks up at the man and says, "Play it? I'm going to shag it as soon as I get its pyjamas off."

The new pet

This guy was lonely, and decided life would be more fun if he had a pet. So he went to the pet store and told the owner that he wanted to buy an unusual pet. After some discussion, he finally bought a centipede, which came in a little white box to use for its house. He took the box back home, found a good location for the box, and decided he would start off by taking his new pet to the bar to have a drink.

He asked the centipede in the box, "Would you like to go to Frank's with me and have a beer?" But there was no answer from his new pet. This bothered him a bit, but he waited a few minutes and then asked him again, "How about going to the bar and having a drink with me?" But again, there was no answer from his new friend and pet.

So he waited a few minutes more, thinking about the situation. He decided to ask him one more time; this time putting his face up against the centipede's house and shouting, "Hey, you in there! Would you like to go to Frank's place and have a drink with me?" A little voice came out of the box: "I heard you the first time! I'm putting on my shoes."

Regional vibe

The cat bronze

One day a northern bloke is walking around the backstreets of London when he comes across a dingy little antiques shop. His curiosity immediately gets the better of him and he goes in for a look round. He notices among the cobwebs and dusty antiquities a pristine bronze statue of a proud looking cat. He thinks it rather unique and takes it to the assistant to enquire about the price.

"Well its £100 for the cat and £1000 for the story that goes with it." replies the assistant.

"I'll tell you what, f*ck the story off an I'll just take the cat."

The deal is done.

After leaving the shop the guys walking down the street with the cat under his arm and he notices a couple of real cats following behind him at a distance. He thinks nothing of it and carries on.

Continuing to walk he realises the number of cats following him is rapidly increasing. More are appearing from each side street he passes and from out of bins and gaps in between the buildings the number continues to increase. He begins to get a little spooked by this and quickens the pace, the cats follow!

He begins a slow jog, the cats do also. At this point he's getting understandably scared and begins a full sprint to try and shake the following felines but they begin to chase. He runs at full pace for a few hundred metres till he comes out from a street and realises he is close to the Thames. The guy has a brainwave and carries on as fast as possible to the river bank. There he launches the cat statue with all the strength he can muster into the murky waters of the Thames. His plan works and the cats follow it. Thousands of them jump to their death chasing the bronze cat.

The man with obvious confusion returns to the shop where he bought the statue and is immediately met by the rather smug cockney with the question, "oh, so I guess now you'd like to hear the story?"

The guy replies, "No thanks, I was just wondering if you had any bronze scousers for sale!" One day a northern bloke is walking around the backstreets of London when he comes across a dingy little antiques shop. His curiosity immediately gets the better of him and he goes in for a look round. He notices among the cobwebs and dusty antiquities a pristine bronze statue of a proud looking cat. He thinks it rather unique and takes it to the assistant to enquire about the price.

"Well its £100 for the cat and £1000 for the story that goes with it." replies the assistant.

"I'll tell you what, f*ck the story off an I'll just take the cat."

The deal is done.

After leaving the shop the guys walking down the street with the cat under his arm and he notices a couple of real cats following behind him at a distance. He thinks nothing of it and carries on.

Continuing to walk he realises the number of cats following him is rapidly increasing. More are appearing from each side street he passes and from out of bins and gaps in between the buildings the number continues to increase. He begins to get a little spooked by this and quickens the pace, the cats follow!

He begins a slow jog, the cats do also. At this point he's getting understandably scared and begins a full sprint to try and shake the following felines but they begin to chase. He runs at full pace for a few hundred metres till he comes out from a street and realises he is close to the Thames. The guy has a brainwave and carries on as fast as possible to the river bank. There he launches the cat statue with all the strength he can muster into the murky waters of the Thames. His plan works and the cats follow it. Thousands of them jump to their death chasing the bronze cat.

The man with obvious confusion returns to the shop where he bought the statue and is immediately met by the rather smug cockney with the question, "oh, so I guess now you'd like to hear the story?"

The guy replies, "No thanks, I was just wondering if you had any bronze scousers for sale!"

Love those Essex girls

An Essex bird goes to the council to register for child benefit.

"How many children"?? asks the council worker.

"10", replies the Essex bird.

"10???" says the council worker.. "What are their names?"

"Wayne, Wayne, Wayne, Wayne, Wayne, Wayne, Wayne, Wayne, Wayne and…Wayne"

"Doesn't that get confusing?"

"Nnaah…" says the Essex bird "It's great because if they are out playing in the street I just have to shout 'WAAAAAYNE, YER DINNERS READY' or 'WAAAAAAYNE GO TO BED NAAAAAH!!' and they all do it…"

"What if you want to speak to one individually?" asks the perturbed council worker.

"That's easy" says the Essex bird ……….."I just use their surnames".

Perfume

Two Essex girls walk up to a perfume counter and pick up a sample bottle. Sharon sprays some on her wrist and smells it.

"That's quite nice innit, don't you fink Trace?"

"Yeah, wot's it called?"

"Viens a Moi"

"VIENS A MOI? Wot the fack does that mean?"

At this stage the assistant offered some help. "Viens a Moi, ladies is French for 'come to me…'"

Sharon takes anther sniff and offers her arm to Tracey again.

"That doesn't smell like cum to me, Trace. Does that smell like cum to you?"

The Irish Section!

Irish Scarecrow

Stay clear of technology

Three men: one American, one Japanese and an Irishman were sitting naked in the sauna.

Suddenly there was a beeping sound. The American pressed his forearm and the beep stopped. The others looked at him questioningly. "That was my pager," he said. "I have a microchip under the skin of my arm."

A few minutes later a phone rang. The Japanese fellow lifted his palm

To his ear. When he finished he explained, "That was my mobile phone. I have a microchip in my hand."

Paddy felt decidedly low-tech. So as not to be outdone, he decided he had to do something just as impressive. He stepped out of the sauna and went to toilet. He returns with a piece of toilet paper hanging from his back side. The others raised their eyebrows. "Will you look at that" says Paddy, I'm getting a fax."

Spanner

Mick was in court for a double murder and the judge said, "You are charged with beating your wife to death with a spanner."

A voice at the back of the courtroom yelled out, "You bastard!"

The judge continued, "You're also charged with beating your daughter to death with a spanner."

Again, the voice at the back of the courtroom yelled out, "You fucking bastard!!!"

The judge stopped, looked at the man in the back of the courtroom, and said, "Paddy, I can understand your anger and frustration at this crime, but I will not have any more of these outbursts from you or I shall charge you with contempt! Now what is the problem?"

Paddy, at the back of the court stood up and responded, "For fifteen years I lived next door to that bastard. And every time I asked to borrow a fucking spanner, he said he didn't have one!"

Great bar

A Scotsman, an Italian, and an Irishman are in a bar. They are having a good time and all agree that the bar is a nice place. Then the Scotsman says, "Aye, this is a nice bar, but where I come from, back in Glasgee, there's a better one. At MacDougal's, ye buy a drink, ye buy another drink, and MacDougal himself will buy yir third drink!" The others agree that sounds like a good place.

Then the Italian says, "Yeah, dat's a nica bar, but where I come from, dere's a better one……. In Roma, dere's this place, Vincenzo's. At Vincenzo's, you buy a drink, Vincenzo buys you a drink. You buy anudda drink, Vincenzo buys you anudda drink." Everyone agrees that sounds like a great bar.

Then the Irishman says, "You tink dat's great? Where Oi come from in Oirland, dere's dis place called Morphy's. At Morphy's, dey boy you your forst drink, dey boy you your second drink, dey boy you your tird drink, and den, dey take you in de back and get you laid!" "Wow!" says the other two. "That's fantastic! Did that actually happen to you?" "No," replies the Irish guy, "but it happened to me sister!"

Naming

An Englishman an Irishman and a Scotsman were in a pub, talking about their sons. "My son was born on St George's Day," commented the Englishman. "So we obviously decided to call him George." "That's a real coincidence," remarked the Scot. "My son was born on

St Andrew's Day, so obviously we decided to call him Andrew." "That's incredible, what a coincidence," said the Irishman. "Exactly the same thing happened with my son Pancake."

Fair cop

An Irishman was drinking at the pub all night. The bartender came up to him and told him that the bar was closing. So the Irishman stood up to leave and fell flat on his face. He tried to stand up one more time with the same result. So he figured he'd just crawl outside, hang out for a while, get some fresh air and hopefully that would sober him up.

Once outside he stood up and fell again right on his face. So he decided to crawl the 4 blocks to his home and when he arrived at the door he tried one more time with the same results. Exhausted, he then gave up and started crawling to the bedroom. When he reached his bed he tried one more time to stand up. This time he managed to pull himself upright but he quickly fell right into the bed and fell sound asleep as soon as his head hit the pillow.

The next morning, he woke up with his wife standing over him shouting at him. "So, you've been out drinking again!!" "What makes you say that?" He asked as he put on an innocent look. "The pub called, you left your wheelchair there again."

Thank you doctor

An Irish bloke goes to the doctor

Dactor, it's me ahrse. I'd loik ya ta teyhk a look, if ya woot.

So the doctor gets him to drop his pants and takes a look. Incredible he says, there is a £20 note lodged up here.

Tentatively he eases the twenty out of the man's bottom, and then a £10 note appears. This is amazing exclaims the Doctor. What do you want me to do?

Well fur gadness sake teyhk it out man shrieks the patient. The doctor pulls out the tenner and another twenty appears, and another and another etc....

Finally the last note comes out and no more appear.

Ah Dactor, tank ya koindly, dat's moch batter, how moch is dare den?

The Doctor counts the pile of cash......£1,990 exactly.

.
.
.
.
.
.

.wait for it....

.
.
.
.
.
.

.Ah, dat'd be roit.

I knew I wasn't feeling two grand!!

The Leprechaun

A man had just finished a putt and reached in the hole to get his ball, but pulled out a leprechaun!

"Sure, and ye have me," cried the leprechaun. "And if you let me go, for yer tribble, I'll give ye three wishes!"

"Thank you," said the man. "I don't really need anything, so I'll pass on the wishes." He let the leprechaun go, and went off to finish his game.

The leprechaun was dumbfounded. Who had ever heard of such a thing? He sat on a pebble and thought to himself "Such a man as that deserves three wishes! I'll give 'em to 'in spite 'imself! Now what should he wish for? Why money, of course! Everyone wants money. So, for his first wish he wants to be a millionaire! And second—let's make him a great golfer! And last—ah! Let him have a wonderful sex life.

A month went by and the leprechaun spotted the man playing on the course again. He jumped out of a hole and yelled up to the man "How ye be doing?"

The man smiled and said "Hello, little friend. I be doing just fine."

The leprechaun smiled back and said "And how's your money situation, if you don't mind my askin'?"

"It's funny you should ask," replied the man. "An uncle of mine passed away and left me a fortune!"

"Hah! Is that so? And how's yer golf game now?"

"It's an amazing thing," said the man. "For the past few weeks I can't do worse than two under par!"

"Sure, and that's wonderful!" With a sly look, the leprechaun asked, "And how's yer sex life?"

The man, obviously embarrassed, looked away and coughed, "Well, it's fine. Two or three times a month."

The leprechaun was aghast. "Two or three times a month? That's horrible!"

The man looked up and said, "Actually, it's not bad for a priest in a small parish."

Opportunist

They sit in the front row next to the stage while Blondie does her stuff.

For the finale she waggles her naked a*se in the Englishman's face;

He reaches for his wallet, takes out a tenner, licks it and slaps it on her left buttock.

The stripper moves along and repeats the manoeuvre in front of the Irishman, he too takes a tenner from his wallet, licks it and slaps

It on her right cheek.

She now confronts the Scot with her pert ass and squashes it in his face. Hysterically he removes his wallet, takes out his Debit card, swipes it between her cheeks; and takes twenty pounds cashback!!!

To see ourselves as others see us

Paddy died in a fire and was burnt pretty bad; the morgue needed someone to identify the body. So his two best friends sent for.

Dermot went in and the mortician pulled back the sheet. Dermot said "Yup, he's burnt pretty bad. Roll him over." So the mortician rolled him over. Dermot looked and said "Nope, it ain't Paddy."

The mortician thought that was rather strange so he brought Tony in to identify the body. Tony took a look at him and said "Yup, he's burnt real bad, roll him over." The mortician rolled him over and Tony looked down and said "No, it ain't Paddy."

The mortician asked "well, how can you tell?" "Well, Paddy had two assholes" said Tony. "What? He had two assholes?" said the mortician. "Yup, everyone knew he had two assholes. Every time we went into town, folks would say: Here comes Paddy with them two assholes"

Don't try this at home

Two Irishmen walk into a pet shop. Right away they go over to the Bird section. Gerry says to Paddy, "Dat's dem." The clerk comes over and asks if he can help them.

"Yeah, we'll take four of dem dere birds in dat cage op dere" says Gerry, "an' put dem in a peeper bag."

The clerk does and the two guys pay for the birds and leave the shop. They get into Gerry's van and drive until they are high up in the hills and stop at the top of a cliff with a 500 foot drop.

"Dis looks loik a grand place, eh?" says Gerry.

He then takes two birds out of the bag, places them on his shoulders and jumps off the cliff. Paddy watches as his mate drops off the edge and goes straight down for a few seconds followed by a 'SPLAT'.

As Paddy looks over the edge of the cliff he shakes his head and says, "Fock dat, dis budgie jumpin' is too fockin' dangerous for me."

A minute later, Seamus arrives. He too has been to the pet shop and he walks up carrying the familiar 'peeper bag'. He pulls a parrot out of the bag, and then Paddy notices that, in his other hand, Seamus is carrying a gun.

"Hi, Paddy. Watch dis," Seamus says and launches himself over the edge of the cliff. Paddy watches as half way down, Seamus takes out the gun and blows the parrot's head off.

Seamus continues to plummet until there is a 'SPLAT'!, as he joins Gerry's remains at the bottom.

Paddy shakes his head and says, "An' oim never troyin' dat parrotshooting nider."

A few minutes after Seamus splats himself Sean strolls up. He too has been to the pet shop and he walks up carrying the familiar 'peeper bag'. Instead of a parrot he pulls a chicken out of the bag, and launches himself off the cliff with the usual result.

Once more Paddy shakes his head - 'Fock me Sean, first der was Gerry wit his budgie jumping, den Seamus parrotshooting and now you fockin' hengliding."

A tale of two pigs

Paddy and Paddy, two Irishmen, went out one day and each bought a pig. When they got home, Paddy turned to Paddy and said "Paddy, me ol' mate, how we gonna tell who owns which fookin pig?"

Paddy says, "Well Paddy, I'll cut one a ta' ears off my fookin pig, and ten we can tell 'em apart." "Ah tat'd be grand." Says Paddy.

This worked fine until a couple of weeks later when Paddy stormed into the house. "Paddy" he said "Your fookin pig has chewed the ear offa my fookin pig. Now we got two fookin pigs with on one ear each. How we gonna tell who owns which fookin pig?"

"Well Paddy" said Paddy "I'll cut ta other ear off my fookin pig. Ten we'll av two fookin pigs and only one of them will avan ear" "Ah tat'd be grand." says Paddy.

Again this worked fine until a couple of weeks later when Paddy again stormed into the house."Paddy" he said "Your fookin pig has chewed the other ear offa my fookin pig. Now we got two fookin pigs with no fookin ears. How we gonna tell who owns which fookin pig?" "Ah tis is serious, Paddy." Said Paddy "I'll tell ya what I'll do I'll cut ta tail offa my fookin pig. Ten we'll av two fookin pigs with no fookin ears and only one fookin tail." "Ah tat'd be grand." says Paddy.

Another couple of weeks went by, and you guessed it, Paddy stormed into the house once more. "PADDY" shouted Paddy "YOUR FOOKIN PIG HAS CHEWED THE FOOKIN TAIL OFFA MY FOOKIN PIG AND NOW WE GOT TWO FOOKIN PIGS WITH NO FOOKIN EARS AND NO FOOKIN TAILS!!!!! HOW THE FOOK ARE WE GONNA FOOKIN TELL 'EM APART!!!!!!!!"

"Ah fook it." Says Paddy "How's about you have the black one, and I'll have the white one?"

The masterpiece

A couple is at an art exhibit in Dublin, and they are looking at a portrait that has them a little taken aback. The picture depicts three very black, very naked men sitting on a park bench.

Two have a black truncheons and the one in the middle has a pink truncheon. As the couple is looking somewhat puzzled at the picture, the Irish artist walks by and says, "Can I help you with this painting? I'm Paddy O'Toole, and this is my latest masterpiece".

The man says "Well, we like the painting but don't understand why you have three African men on a bench and the one in the middle has a pink truncheon while the other two have a black truncheons."

The Irish artist says "Oh, you are misinterpreting the painting. They're not African men. They are Irish coal miners and the one in the middle went home for lunch."

It's a girl!

A pregnant Irish woman from Dublin was in a car accident and fell into a deep coma. The coma continued for nearly 6 months, but then she suddenly woke up, alarmed to find that she was no longer pregnant. Frantic, she asked the doctor about her baby.

The doctor replied, "You had twins! A boy and a girl. Your brother from Cork came in and named them."

This caused the woman some concern, with the thought - 'Oh no, not my brother...he's an idiot!' - flashing through her mind. With some trepidation, she asked the doctor, "Well, what's the girl's name?"

"Denise."

"Wow, that's not a bad name, I like it! What's the boy's name?"

"Denephew."

Consultants

Modern day man

A shepherd was herding his flock in a remote pasture when suddenly a brand-new BMW advanced out of a dust cloud towards him. The driver, a young man in a Broni suit, Gucci shoes, Ray Ban sunglasses and YSL tie, leans out the window and asks the shepherd, "If I tell you exactly how many sheep you have in your flock, will you let me take one?"

The shepherd looks at the obvious yuppie, then looks at his peacefully grazing flock and calmly answers, "Sure. Why not?" The yuppie parks his car, whips out his Dell notebook computer,

Connects it to his AT&T cell phone, surfs to a NASA page on the internet, where he calls up a GPS satellite navigation system to get an exact fix on his

Location which he then feeds to another NASA satellite that scans the area in an ultra-high-resolution photo. They young man then opens the digital photo in Adobe Photoshop and exports it to an image processing facility in Hamburg, Germany. Within seconds, he receives an email on his Palm Pilot that the image has been processed and the data stored. He then accesses a MS-SQL database through an ODBC connected Excel spreadsheet with hundreds of complex formulas. He uploads all of this data via an email on his Blackberry and, after a few minutes, receives a response.

Finally, he prints out a full-colour, 150-page report on his hi-tech, miniaturized HP LaserJet printer and finally turns to the shepherd and says, "You have exactly 1586 sheep." "That's right. Well, I guess you can take one of my sheep," says the shepherd. He watches the young man select one of the animals and looks on amused as the young man stuffs it into the trunk of his car.

Then the shepherd says to the young man, "Hey, if I can tell you exactly what your business is, will you give me back my sheep?"

The young man thinks about it for a second and then says, "Okay, why not?" "You're an IT consultant." says the shepherd. "Wow! That's correct," says the yuppie, "but how did you guess that?"

"No guessing required." answered the shepherd. "You showed up here even though nobody called you; you want to get paid for an answer I already knew; to a question I never asked; and you don't know crap about my business"

"Now give me back my dog."

The power of letters

From a strictly mathematical viewpoint it goes like this: What Makes 100%?

What does it mean to give MORE than 100%? Ever wonder about those people who say they are giving more than 100%? We have all been to those meetings where someone wants you to give over 100%. How about achieving 103%? Here's a little mathematical formula that might help you answer these questions: What makes up 100% in life?

If:

A B C D E F G H I J K L M N O P Q R S T U V W X Y Z

is represented as:

1 2 3 4 5 6 7 8 9 10 11 12 13 14 15 16 17 18 19 20 21 22 23 24 25 26.

Then:

H-A-R-D-W-O-R-K

$8+1+18+4+23+15+18+11 = 98\%$

and

K-N-O-W-L-E-D-G-E

$11+14+15+23+12+5+4+7+5 = 96\%$

But,

A-T-T-I-T-U-D-E

$1+20+20+9+20+21+4+5 = 100\%$

And…,

B-U-L-L-S-H-I-T

$2+21+12+12+19+8+9+20 = 103\%$

Look how far ass kissing will take you. A-S-S-K-I-S-S-I-N-G!

$1+19+19+11+9+19+19+9+14+7 = 118\%$

So, one can then conclude with mathematical certainty that: While hard work and knowledge will get you close, Attitude will get you there, Bullshit and Ass kissing will put you over the top.

The art of Management

Management Lessons
Lesson One

An eagle was sitting on a tree resting, doing nothing. A small rabbit saw the eagle & asked him, "Can I also sit like you & do nothing?" The eagle answered: "Sure, why not." So, the rabbit sat on the ground below the eagle, and rested. All of a sudden, a fox appeared, jumped on the rabbit and ate it.

Management Lesson?

To be sitting and doing nothing, you must be sitting very, very high up.

Lesson Two

A turkey was chatting with a bull. "I would love to be able to get to the top of that tree," sighed the turkey, "but I haven't got the energy." "Well, why don't you nibble on some of my droppings?" replied the bull. "They're packed with nutrients." The turkey pecked at a lump of dung, found it actually gave him enough strength to reach the lowest branch of the tree. The next day, after eating some more dung, he reached the second branch. Finally after a fourth night, he was proudly perched at the top of the tree. Soon he was promptly spotted by a farmer, who shot the turkey out of the tree.

Management Lesson?

Bullshit might get you to the top, but it won't keep you there.

Lesson Three

A little bird was flying south for the winter. It was so cold the bird froze and fell to the ground in a large field. While it was lying there, a cow came by and dropped some dung on it. As the frozen bird lay there in the pile of cow dung, it began to realize how warm it was. The dung was actually thawing him out! He lay there all warm and happy, and soon began to sing for joy. A passing cat heard the bird singing and came to investigate. Following the sound, the cat discovered the bird under the pile of cow dung, and promptly dug him out and ate him.

Management Lesson?

1) Not everyone who shits on you is your enemy.
2) Not everyone who gets you out of shit is your friend.
3) And when you're in deep shit, it's best to keep your mouth shut!

Lesson 4

A Sales Rep., an Administration Clerk and the Manager are walking to lunch when they find an antique oil lamp. They rub it and a Genie comes out in a puff of smoke. The Genie says, "I usually only grant three wishes, so I'll give you just one each"W.

"Me first, me first" says the Admin. Clerk. "I want to be in the Bahamas, driving a speedboat, without a care in the world". Poof! She's gone.

The astonished Sales Rep shouts "Me next! me next! I want to be in Hawaii, relaxing on the beach with my personal masseuse, an endless supply of Pina Coladas and the love of my life". Poof! He's gone.

"OK, you're up" the Genie says to the Manager. "I want those two back in the office after lunch" says the Manager.

Moral of the Story: Always let your boss have the first say!

Driving

Road signs

> PLEASE DRIVE SAFELY
>
> UNMARKED NUCLEAR WARHEADS TRAVEL THESE ROADS
>
> KEEP OUR CHILDREN RADIATION-FREE!

Erk!

THE GREATEST JOKE COMPENDIUM OF ALL TIME — FOR OUR TIMES

In case Batman gets lost, presumably.

Decisions, decisions!

COMPILED BY ROY VEGA

Only 36% of women ever find this.

…..obviously.

Harsh methods of population control.

THE GREATEST JOKE COMPENDIUM OF ALL TIME — FOR OUR TIMES

Hurrah!

Yes, well, err……?

Hope it's not urgent.

Tasty.

Prince Phillip says much the same.

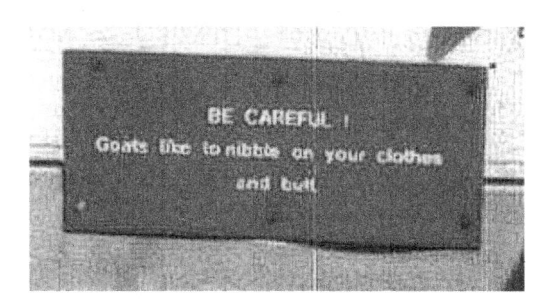

Not on the first date, though.

= "You're shagged".

So make sure it's on your CV.

THE GREATEST JOKE COMPENDIUM OF ALL TIME — FOR OUR TIMES

Hygiene is important.

It's a dream come true.

McDeath?

Spoilsports.

Not even an emergency phone.

THE GREATEST JOKE COMPENDIUM OF ALL TIME — FOR OUR TIMES

To chill out those stressed rabbits.

Obviously an American sign.

Ooops.

COMPILED BY ROY VEGA

Another dream come true….

What exactly is the alternative to "While U Wait?

Such insight……

Sexist – plain & simple

New cash machines

The Building Society is very pleased to announce that they are installing new "Drive Thru" Cash Dispensers. To enable customers to gain maximum benefit from this new facility they have conducted intensive behavioural studies to come up with the appropriate procedures for their use. AS FOLLOWS:

Procedures for MALE customers
1. Drive up to the cash machine
2. Wind down your car window
3. Insert your card into machine and enter PIN
4. Enter amount of cash required and withdraw
5. Retrieve card, cash, and receipt
6. Wind up window
7. Drive off

Procedures for FEMALE customers
1. Drive up to the cash machine

2. Reverse the required distance to align car window with cash machine
3. Re-start the stalled engine
4. Wind down the window
5. Find handbag, remove all contents onto passenger seat to find card
6. Turn the radio down
7. Attempt to insert card into machine
8. Open car door to allow easier access to cash machine due to its excessive distance from the car
9. Insert card
10. Re-insert card the right way up
11. Re-enter handbag to find diary with your PIN number written on the inside back page
12. Enter PIN
13. Press "cancel" and re-enter correct PIN
14. Enter amount of cash required
15. Check make-up in rear view mirror
16. Retrieve cash and receipt
17. Empty handbag again to locate purse and place cash inside
18. Place receipt in back of cheque book
19. Re-check make-up
20. Drive forward 2 metres
21. Reverse back to cash machine
22. Retrieve card
23. Re-empty handbag, locate card holder, and place card into slot provided
24. Restart stalled engine and pull off
25. Drive for 2 to 3 miles

26. Release handbrake.

OR YOU CAN JUST GIVE YOUR CARD TO A MAN

The male view

How many men does it take to open a beer?
None. ** It should be opened by the time she brings it.

Why is a Laundromat a really bad place to pick up a woman?
Because a woman who can't even afford a washing machine will probably never be able to support you.

Why do women have smaller feet than men?
It's one of those "evolutionary things" that allows them to stand closer to the kitchen sink.

How do you know when a woman is about to say something smart?
When she starts her sentence with "A man once told me…"

How do you fix a woman's watch?
You don't.. There is a clock on the oven.

Why do men break wind more than women?
Because women can't shut up long enough to build up the required pressure.

If your dog is barking at the back door and your wife is yelling at the front door, who do you let in first?

The dog, of course. He'll shut up once you let him in.

What's worse than a Male Chauvinist Pig?
A woman who won't do what she's told.

I married Miss Right.
I just didn't know her first name was Always.

I haven't spoken to my wife for 18 months: I don't like to interrupt her.

Scientists have discovered a food that diminishes a woman's sex drive by 90%. It's called a Wedding Cake.

Our last fight was my fault: My wife asked me "What's on the TV?"
I said, "Dust!"

In the beginning, God created the earth and rested.*
Then God created Man and rested. Then God created Woman.*
Since then, neither God nor Man has rested.

Why do men die before their wives?*
They want to.

THE GREATEST JOKE COMPENDIUM OF ALL TIME — FOR OUR TIMES

A beggar walked up to a well-dressed woman shopping on Rodeo Drive and said, "I haven't eaten anything for days." She looked at him and said,* "God, I wish I had your willpower."

Young Son: "Is it true, Dad, I heard that in some parts of Africa a man doesn't know his wife until he marries her?"
Dad: * "That happens in every country, son."*

A man inserted an advertisement in the classified: Wife Wanted." The next day he received a hundred letters. *
They all said the same thing: "You can have mine."

Most effective way to remember your wife's birthday is to forget it once.

Women will never be equal to men until they can walk down the street with a bald head and a beer gut, and still think they are beautiful.

Showering

How to shower like a woman….
1. Take off clothing and place it in sectioned laundry hamper according to lights and darks.
2. Walk to bathroom wearing long dressing gown. If you see your boyfriend/husband along the way, cover up any exposed flesh and rush to bathroom.

3. Look at your womanly physique in the mirror and stick out your gut so that you can complain and whine even more about how you're getting fat.
4. Get in the shower. Look for facecloth, arm cloth, leg cloth, long loofah, wide loofah and pumice stone.
5. Wash your hair once with Cucumber and Lamfrey shampoo with 83 added vitamins.
6. Wash your hair again with Cucumber and Lamfrey shampoo with 83 added vitamins.
7. Condition your hair with Cucumber and Lamfrey conditioner enhanced with natural crocus oil. Leave on hair for 15 minutes.
8. Wash your face with crushed apricot facial scrub for ten minutes until red raw.
9. Wash entire rest of body with Ginger Nut and Jaffa Cake body wash.
10. Rinse conditioner off hair (this takes at least 15 minutes as you must make sure that it has all come off).
11. Shave armpits and legs. Consider shaving bikini area but decide to get it waxed instead.
12. Scream loudly when your boyfriend/husband flushes the toilet and you lose the water pressure.
13. Turn off the shower.
14. Squeegee off all wet surfaces in shower. Spray mould spots with Tilex.

15. Get out of shower. Dry with towel the size of a small African country. Wrap hair in super absorbent second towel.
16. Check entire body for the remotest sign of a zit. Attack with nails/tweezers if found.
17. Return to bedroom wearing long dressing gown and towel on head.
18. If you see your boyfriend/husband along the way, cover up any exposed flesh and then rush to bedroom to spend an hour and a half getting dressed.

How to shower like a man…
1. Take off clothes while sitting on the edge of the bed and leave them in a pile.
2. Walk naked to the bathroom. If you see your girlfriend/wife along the way, flash her making the "woo" sound.
3. Look at your manly physique in the mirror and suck in your gut to see if you have pecs (no). Admire the size of your dick in the mirror, scratch your balls and smell your fingers for one last whiff.
4. Get in the shower.
5. Don't bother to look for a washcloth. (You don't use one).
6. Wash your face.
7. Wash your armpits.
8. Crack up at how loud your fart sounds in the shower.

9. Wash your privates and surrounding area. Continually.
10. Wash your arse, leaving hair on the soap bar.
11. Shampoo your hair. (do not use conditioner).
12. Make a shampoo Mohawk.
13. Pull back shower curtain and look at yourself in the mirror.
14. Pee (in the shower)
15. Rinse off and get out of the shower. Fail to notice water on the floor because you left the curtain hanging out of the tub the whole time.
16. Partial dry off.
17. Look at yourself in the mirror, flex muscles. Admire dick size.
18. Leave shower curtain open and wet bath mat on the floor.
19. Leave bathroom light and fan on.
20. Return to the bedroom with towel around your waist. If you pass your girlfriend/wife, pull off the towel, grab your dick, go "yeah baby" and thrust your pelvis at her.
21. Throw wet towel on the bed. Take 2 minutes to get dressed

Ergonomic mouse

Given the difficulties with the utilisation of the standard mouse experienced by women, IBM and Microsoft have joined forces to try to find a solution to the problem.

THE GREATEST JOKE COMPENDIUM OF ALL TIME — FOR OUR TIMES

Both companies, after many years of research and experimentation into the needs of women of all ages, have created a new mouse (ergonomically designed for female hands) and it has already had a great impact among the female population of computer users, finally ending years of problems caused by previous designs.

Introducing the new 'Mouse for Women'....

Woman driver

Last weekend, Saturday afternoon to be exact, a woman wanted to go shopping at Galeries Lafayette in Paris. Finding it difficult to park in the busy streets adjacent to the shop, she decided to make for the underground car-park. Unfortunately, the underground "car-park" was instead the entrance to the metro. (See picture) Unbelievably, she wasn't even fined, but at least no-one was injured.

Work – Pah!

Oops

I lost my job today.

I came into work on time…..I did exactly what the boss told me to do! I followed all the rules, and never once disrespected anybody…

Then, the first time I ever had a chance to drive one of them fork lifts, I made one little mistake, and everyone starts running around in circles screaming and shouting. You'd think I blew the place up or something, the way people were looking at me afterwards!

I don't understand it….I didn't mean to do it…It was an accident….Everyone messes up, it could've happened to anyone

Misunderstanding

A new employee is hired at the Tickle Me Elmo factory. The personnel manager explains her duties and tells her to report to work promptly at 8:00am.

The next day at 8:45am, there's a knock at the personnel manager's door.

The assembly line foreman comes in and starts ranting about this new employee. He says she's incredibly slow, and the whole line is backing up.

The foreman takes the personnel manager down to the factory floor to show him the problem. Sure enough, Elmos are backed up all over the place. At the end of the line is the new employee. She has a roll of the material used for the Elmos and a big bag of marbles. They both watch as she cuts a little piece of fabric, wraps it around two marbles, and starts sewing the little package between Elmo's legs.

The personnel manager starts laughing hysterically. After several minutes, he pulls himself together, walks over to the woman, and says, I'm sorry, I guess you misunderstood me yesterday. "Your job is to give Elmo two test tickles."

Parental wisdom

Lessons taught by Mum

MUM TAUGHT ME TO APPRECIATE A JOB WELL DONE —
"If you're going to kill each other, do it outside, I just finished cleaning!"

MUM TAUGHT ME RELIGION —
"You better pray that will come out of that carpet!"

MUM TAUGHT ME ABOUT TIME TRAVEL —
"If you don't straighten up, I'll knock you into next week!"

MUM TAUGHT ME LOGIC —
"Because I said so, that's why!"

MUM TAUGHT ME FORESIGHT —
"Make sure you wear clean underwear in case you're in an accident."

MUM TAUGHT ME IRONY —
"Keep laughing and I'll give you something to cry about!"

MUM TAUGHT ME ABOUT THE SCIENCE OF OSMOSIS —
"Shut your mouth and eat your supper!"

MUM TAUGHT ME ABOUT CONTORTIONISM —
"Will you look at the dirt on the back of your neck?"

MUM TAUGHT ME ABOUT STAMINA —
"You'll sit there until all that spinach is gone!"

MUM TAUGHT ME ABOUT WEATHER —
"It looks like a tornado went through your room!"

MUM TAUGHT ME HOW TO SOLVE PHYSICS PROBLEMS —
"If I yelled because I saw a meteor coming toward you, would you listen then?"

MUM TAUGHT ME ABOUT HYPOCRISY —
"If I told you once, I've told you a million times — don't exaggerate!"

MUM TAUGHT ME ABOUT BEHAVIOUR MODIFICATION —
"Stop acting like your father!"

MUM TAUGHT ME ABOUT ENVY —
"There are millions of less fortunate kids in this world who don't have wonderful parents like you do!"

MUM TAUGHT ME ORTHOPAEDICS —
"If you fall out of that tree and break both of your legs, don't come running to me!"

And most of all ..

MUM TAUGHT ME THE CIRCLE OF LIFE —
"I brought you into this world, I can take you out!"

Careful of my daughter!

A young man was wandering, lost, in a forest when he came upon a small house. Knocking on the door he was greeted by an ancient Chinese man with a long, grey beard.

"I'm lost," said the man. "Can you put me up for the night?"

"Certainly," the Chinese man said, "but on one condition. If you so much as lay a finger on my daughter I will inflict upon you the three worst Chinese tortures known to man."

"OK," said the man, thinking that the daughter must be pretty old as well, and entered the house. Before dinner the daughter came down the stairs. She was young, beautiful and had a fantastic figure. She was obviously attracted to the young man as she couldn't keep her eyes off him during the meal.

Remembering the old man's warning he ignored her and went up to bed alone. But during the night he could bear it no longer and sneaked into her room for a night of passion. He was careful to keep everything quiet so the old man wouldn't hear and, near dawn, he crept back to his room, exhausted but happy. He woke to feel a pressure on his chest. Opening his eyes he saw a large rock on his chest with a note on it that read,

"Chinese Torture 1: Large rock on chest."

"Well, that's pretty crappy," he thought. "If that's the best the old man can do then I don't have much to worry about."

He picked the boulder up, walked over to the window and threw the boulder out. As he did so he noticed another note on it that read

"Chinese Torture 2: Rock tied to left testicle."

In a panic he glanced down and saw the rope that was already getting close to taut. Figuring that a few broken bones was better than castration, he jumped out of the window after the boulder. As he plummeted downward he saw a large sign on the ground that read, "Chinese Torture 3: Right testicle tied to bedpost."

Commentating is not easy you know!

Foot in mouth

MICHAEL Buerk watching Phillipa Forrester cuddle up to a male astronomer for warmth during BBC1's UK eclipse coverage remarked: "They seem cold out there, they're rubbing each other and he's only come in his shorts."

Ken Brown commentating on golfer Nick Faldo and his caddie Fanny Sunneson lining-up shots at the Scottish Open: "Some weeks Nick likes to use Fanny, other weeks he prefers to do it by himself."

MIKE Hallett discussing missed snooker shots on Sky Sports: "Stephen Hendry jumps on Steve Davis's misses every chance he gets."

JACK Burnicle was talking about Colin Edwards' tyre choice on World Superbike racing: "Colin had a hard on in practice earlier, and I bet he wished he had a hard on now."

Chris Tarrant discussing the first Millionaire winner Judith Keppel on This Morning: "She was practising fastest finger first by herself in bed last night."

WINNING Post's Stewart Machin commentating on jockey Tony McCoy's formidable lead: "Tony has a quick look between his legs and likes what he sees."

ROSS King discussing relays with champion runner Phil Redmond: "Well Phil, tell us about your amazing third leg."

DURING the 1989 British Masters golf tournament, commentator Richie Benaud observed: "Notices are appearing at courses telling golfers not to lick their balls on the green."

CRICKETER Neil Fairbrother hit a single during a Durham v Lancashire match, inspiring Bobby Simpson to observe: "With his lovely soft hands he just tossed it off."

CLAIR Frisby talking about a jumbo hot dog on Look North said: "There's nothing like a big hot sausage inside you on a cold night like this."

JAMES Allen interviewing Ralf Schumacher at a Grand Prix, asked: "What does it feel like being rammed up the backside by Barrichello?"

STEVE Ryder covering the US Masters: "Ballesteros felt much better today after a 69."

THE new stand at Doncaster race course took Brough Scott's breath away..."My word," he said. "Look at that magnificent erection."

WILLIE Carson was telling Claire Balding how jockeys prepare for a big race when he said: "They usually have four or five dreams a night about coming from different positions."

STEVE Leonard, talking about vegetation on Vets In The Wild, told Trude: "There's something big growing between my legs."

CARENZA Lewis about finding food in the Middle Ages on Time Team Live said: "You'd eat beaver if you could get it."

Boat race chappie "Princess Anne is now kissing the cox of the Cambridge team"

RAY FRENCH on a young Elery Hanley "Ay up the darkies got it and he's gone. They'll not catch him he's like sh1t off shovel."

Toilet Humour

Good Afternoon

This bloke walks into a public toilet where he finds two cubicles, one is already occupied. So he enters the other one, closes the door, drops 'em and sits down. A voice then comes from the cubicle next to him "G'day mate, how are you going?" Thinking this a bit strange but not wanting to be rude the guy replies "Yeh, not to bad thanks"

After a short pause, he hears the voice again "So, what are you up to mate?

Again answering reluctantly, but unsure what to say, replies "Amm, just having a quick poo. How about yourself?"

He then hears the voice for the 3rd time

"Sorry mate, I'll have to call you back, I've got some dickhead next to me answering all my questions"

Bathroom Scribble - pearls of wisdom from around the world

Friends don't let friends take home ugly men

The best way to a man's heart is to saw his breast plate open

Beauty is only a light switch away.

I've decided that to raise my grades I must lower my standards.

If life is a waste of time, and time is a waste of life, then let's all get wasted together and have the time of our lives.

Remember, it's not, "How high are you?" it's "Hi, how are you?"

Fighting for peace is like screwing for virginity.

No matter how good she looks, some other guy is sick and tired of putting up with her crap.

At the feast of ego everyone leaves hungry.

It's hard to make a comeback when you haven't been anywhere

God is dead. – Nietzsche. Nietzsche is dead. - God

If voting could really change things, it would be illegal. .

A Woman's Rule of Thumb: If it has tires or testicles, you're going to have trouble with it.

Express Lane: Five beers or less Sign over one of the urinals in a gents loo.

You're too good for him. Sign over mirror in Women's toilet

No wonder you always go home alone. Sign over mirror in Men's toilet

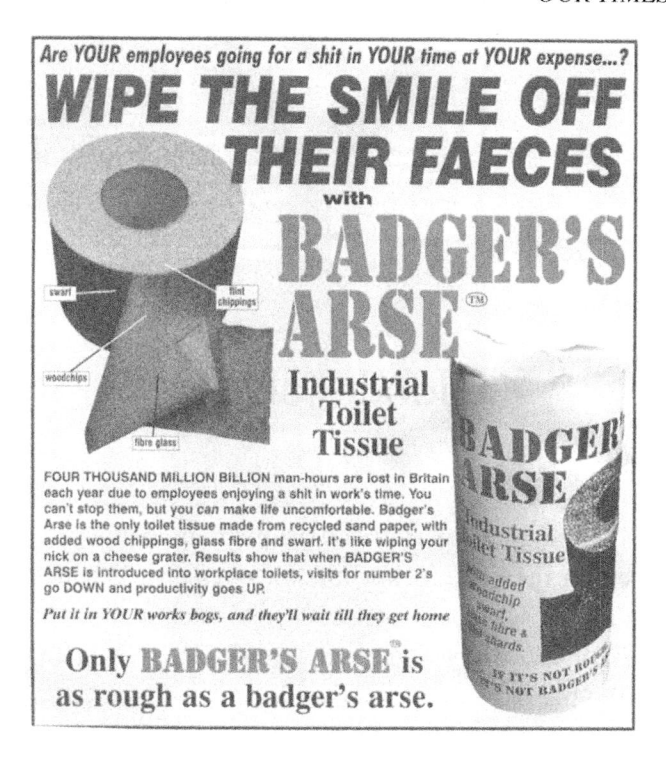

THE GREATEST JOKE COMPENDIUM OF ALL TIME — FOR OUR TIMES

Blonde Jokes

Message Centre

1. A blonde went into a worldwide message centre to send a message to her mother overseas. When the man told her it would cost £300, she exclaimed:

"'But I don't have any money! I'd do ANYTHING to get a message to my mother."

The man arched an eyebrow (as we would expect) and asked, "Anything?"

"Yes! Yes, anything," the blond promised.

"Well then, just follow me," said the man as he walked towards the next room. The blonde did as she was told and followed the man. "Come in and close the door," the man said. She did.

He then said, "Now, get on your knees." She did.

"Now take down my zipper." She did. "Now go ahead, take it out," he said. She reached in and grabbed it with both hands, then paused.

The man closed his eyes and whispered, "Well, go ahead."

The blonde slowly brought her mouth closer to it and while holding it close to her lips, tentatively said,

"Hello! Mom, can you hear me?"

He's right you know

A blind man enters a ladies' bar by mistake. He finds his way to a bar stool and orders a drink. After sitting there for a while, he yells to the bartender, "Hey you wanna hear a blonde joke?" The bar immediately falls absolutely quiet. In a very deep, husky voice, the woman next to the blind man says,

"Before you tell that joke, sir, I think it is only fair — given that you are blind — that you should know 5 things:

"1. The bartender is a blond girl.

"2. The bouncer is a blond girl.

"3. I'm a blonde woman with a black belt in karate.

"4. The woman sitting next to me is a blonde and a weight lifter.

"5. The lady to your right is a blonde and a professional wrestler.

"Now think about it seriously, Mister. Do you still want to tell that joke?"

The blind man thinks for a second, shakes his head and declares, "Nah, not if I'm going to have to explain it five times."

The Mechanic

A few days ago I was having some work done at my local garage. A blonde came in and asked for a seven-hundred-ten. We all looked at each other and another customer asked, "What is a seven-hundred-ten?"

She replied, "You know, the little piece in the middle of the engine, I have lost it and need a new one." She replied that she did not know, but this piece had always been there. He gave her a piece of paper and a pen and asked her to draw what the piece looked like. She drew a circle and in the middle of it wrote 710.

He then took her over to another car that had the hood up and asked

"is there a 710 on this car?". She pointed and said, "Of course, it's right there."

Priceless

A blonde was driving down the motorway when her car phone rang. It was her husband, urgently warning her,

"Honey, I just heard on the news that there's a car going the wrong way on the M25. Please be careful!"

"It's not just one car!" said the blonde, "There's fucking hundreds of them!"

Flowers

Two friends, a blonde and a redhead, are walking down the street and pass a flower shop where the redhead happens to sees her boyfriend buying flowers.

She sighs and says, "Oh, no, my boyfriend is buying me flowers again". The blonde looks quizzically at her and says, 'You don't like getting flowers?'

The redhead says, 'I love getting flowers, but he always has expectations after giving me flowers, and I just don't feel like spending the next three days on my back with my legs in the air.

'The blonde says, 'Don't you have a vase?

Overweight Blonde

A blonde is overweight, so her doctor puts her on a diet.

"I want you to eat regularly for two days, then skip a day, and repeat this procedure for two weeks. The next time I see you, you'll have lost at least five pounds."

When the blonde returns, she's lost nearly 20 pounds.

"Why, that's amazing!" the doctor says.

"Did you follow my instructions?" The blonde nods.

"I'll tell you, though, I thought I was going to drop dead that third day."

"From hunger, you mean?" asked the doctor.
"No, from all that skipping."

Exposure

A blonde is walking down the street with her blouse open and her right breast hanging out. A policeman approaches her and says, "Ma'am, are you aware that I could cite you for indecent exposure?"

She says, "Why, officer?"

"Because your breast is hanging out."

She looks down and says, "OH MY GOD, I left the baby on the bus again!"

River Walk

There's this blonde out for a walk. She comes to a river and sees another blonde on the opposite bank.

"Yoo-hoo" she shouts, "how can I get to the other side?"

The second blonde looks up the river then down the river then shouts back, "You are on the other side."

Knitting

A highway patrolman pulled alongside a speeding car on the freeway. Glancing at the car, he was astounded to see that the blonde behind the wheel was knitting!

Realizing that she was oblivious to his flashing lights and siren, the trooper cranked down his window, turned on his pullhorn and yelled, "PULLOVER!"

"NO," the blonde yelled back, "IT'S A SCARF!"

Blonde on the Sun

A Russian, an American, and a Blonde were talking one day.

The Russian said, "We were the first in space!"

The American said, "We were the first on the moon!"

The Blonde said, "So what, we're going to be the first on the sun!"

The Russian and the American looked at each other and shook their heads.

"You can't land on the sun, you idiot! You'll burn up!" said the Russian.

To which the Blonde replied, "We're not stupid, you know. We're going at night!"

Speeding Ticket

A police officer stops a blonde for speeding and asks her very nicely if he could see her license.

She replied in a huff, "I wish you guys would get your act together. Just yesterday you take away my license and then today you expect me to show it to you!"

The Vacuum

A blonde was playing Trivial Pursuit one night. It was her turn. She rolled the dice and she landed on "Science & Nature." Her question was, "If you are in a vacuum and someone calls your name, can you hear it?"

She thought for a time and then asked, "Is it on or off?"

Final Exam

The blonde reported for her university final examination that consists of "yes/no" type questions. She takes her seat in the examination hall, stares at the question paper for five minutes, and then in a fit of inspiration takes her purse out, removes a coin and starts tossing the coin and marking the answer sheet

"Yes" for Heads and "No" for Tails.

Within half an hour she is all done, whereas the rest of the class is sweating it out.

During the last few minutes, she is seen desperately throwing the coin, muttering and sweating. The moderator, alarmed, approaches her and asks what is going on. "I finished the exam in half an hour, but I'm rechecking my answers."

The Blonde Joke to End All Blonde Jokes!

There was a blonde woman who was having financial troubles so she decided to kidnap a child and demand a ransom. She went to a local park, grabbed a little boy, took him behind a tree and wrote this note. "I have kidnapped your child. Leave $10,000 in a plain brown bag behind the big oak tree in the park tomorrow at 7am

Signed,

The Blonde"

She pinned the note inside the little boy's jacket and told him to go straight home.

The next morning, she returned to the park to find the $10,000 in a brown bag, behind the big oak tree, just as she had instructed. Inside the bag was the following note… "Here is your money. I cannot believe that one blonde would do this to another!"

It's hereditary

A young little blond girl comes back from school one evening.

She runs to her mum and says: "Mummy today at school we learnt how to count.

Well, all the other girls only counted to 5, but listen to me:

1,2,3,4,5,6,7,8,9,10! It's good, innit?"

"Yes darling, very good."

"Is that because I'm blond?"

"Yes darling, it's because you're blond."

Next day, the little girl comes back from school and says: "Mummy, today at school we learnt the alphabet. All the other girls only went as far as D, but listen to me: A, B, C, D, E, F, G, H, I, J, K! It's good "innit?"

"Yes darling, very good."

"Is that because I'm blond, mummy?"

"Yes darling it's because you're blond."

Next Day, she returns from school and cries:

"Mummy, today we went swimming. Well, all the other girls have no breasts, but look at me!"

She proceeds to flash her impressive 36 D at her mummy.

"Is that because I'm blond, mummy?"

"No darling, it's because you're 25."

The Ventriloquist

A young ventriloquist is touring the clubs and stops to entertain at a bar in a small town. He's going through his usual run of stupid blonde jokes, when a big blond woman in the fourth row stands on her chair and says:

"I've heard just about enough of your denigrating blonde jokes, Arsehole.

What makes you think you can stereotype women that way?

What does a person's physical attributes have to do with their worth as a human being?

It's blokes like you who keep women like me from being respected at work and in my community, of reaching my full potential as a person …because you and your kind continue to perpetuate discrimination against not only blondes but women at large …all in the name of humour".

Flustered, the ventriloquist starts to apologise, when the blonde pipes up, "You fucking stay out of this Mister, I'm talking to the little bastard on your knee!"

Age

Thought for the Day

There is more money being spent on breast implants and Viagra than Alzheimers research.

This means that by 2020, there should be a large elderly population with perky boobs and huge erections and absolutely no recollection of what to do with them.

Ethel's Wheelchair

Ethel is a bit of a demon in her wheelchair, and loves to charge around the nursing home, taking corners on one wheel and getting up to maximum speed on the long corridors. Because she and her fellow residents are one sandwich short of a picnic, they all tolerate each other some of the males actually join in.

One day, Ethel was speeding up one corridor when a door opened and Mad Mike stepped out of his room with his arm outstretched. "STOP!" he said in a firm voice. "Have you got a license for that thing?"

Ethel fished around in her handbag and pulled out a Kit Kat wrapper and held it up to him.

OK" he said, and away Ethel sped down the hall.

As she took the corner near the TV lounge on one wheel, Weird William popped out in front of her and shouted, "STOP! Have you got proof of insurance?" Ethel dug into her handbag, pulled out a beer coaster and held it up to him.

William nodded and said, "Carry on, ma'am."

As Ethel neared the final corridor before the front door, Bonkers Brian stepped out in front of her, stark naked, holding a very sizable for his age) erection in his hand.

Oh, no!" said Ethel, "Not the breathalyser again."

Court Appearance

Defence Attorney: What is your age?

Little old Woman: I am 86 years old.

Defence Attorney: Will you tell us, in your own words, what happened to you?

Little old Woman: There I was, sitting there in my swing on my front porch on a warm spring evening, when a young man comes creeping up on the porch and sat down beside me.

Defence Attorney: Did you know him?

Little old Woman: No, but he sure was friendly.

Defence Attorney: What happened after he sat down?

Little old Woman: He started to rub my thigh.

Defence Attorney: Did you stop him?

Little old Woman: No, I didn't stop him.

Defence Attorney: Why not?

Little old Woman: It felt good. Nobody had done that since my Abner passed away some 30 years ago.

Defence Attorney: What happened next?

Little old Woman: He began to rub my breasts.

Defence Attorney: Did you stop him then?

Little old Woman: No, I did not stop him.

Defence Attorney: Why not?

Little old Woman: Why, Your Honour, his rubbing made me feel all alive and excited. I haven't felt that good in years!

Defence Attorney: What happened next?

Little old Woman: Well, I was feeling so spicy that I just laid down and said to him…"Take me …young man…Take me!"

Defence Attorney: Did he take you?

Little old Woman: Hell, no. He just yelled, "April Fools!"…..And that's when I shot the little bastard………

You know you are getting old when………..

1. You leave gigs before the encore to "beat the rush"
2. You own a lawnmower
3. You stop dreaming of becoming a professional footballer and start dreaming of having a son who might instead.
4. Before throwing the local paper away, you look through the property section
5. You prefer Later with Jools Holland to Top of the Pops

6. All of a sudden, Tony Blair is not 46, he's only 46.
7. Before going out anywhere, you ask what the parking is like
8. Flicking through Heat magazine makes you too tired to go out
9. Rather than throw a knackered pair of trainers out, you keep them because they'll be all right for the garden
10. You buy your first ever T-shirt without anything written on it.
11. Instead of laughing at the innovations catalogue that falls out of the newspaper, you suddenly see both the benefit and money saving properties of a plastic winter cover for your garden bench and an electronic mole repellent for the lawn. Not to mention the plastic man for the car to deter would- be thieves.
12. You start to worry about your parents' health.
14. Sure, you have more disposable income, but everything you want to buy costs between 200 and 500 quid.
15. You don't get funny looks when you buy a Disney video or a Wallace and Gromit bubble bath, as the sales assistant assumes they are for your child.
16. Pop music all starts to sound crap.
17. You opt for Pizza Express over Pizza Hut because they don't have any pictures on the menus and anyway, they do a really nice half-bottle of house white.

THE GREATEST JOKE COMPENDIUM OF ALL TIME — FOR OUR TIMES

18. You become powerless to resist the lure of self-assembly furniture.
19. You always have enough milk in
20. To compensate for the fact that you have little desire to go clubbing, you instead frequent really loud tapas restaurants and franchise pubs with wacky names in the mistaken belief that you have not turned into your parents
21. While flicking through the TV channels, you happen upon C4's Time Team with Tony Robinson. You get drawn in.
22. The benefits of a pension scheme become clear
23. You go out of your way to pick up a colour chart from B&Q
24. You wish you had a shed
25. You have a shed
26. You actually find yourself saying, "They don't make 'em like that anymore" and "I remember when there were only 3 TV channels" and "Of Course, in my day…."
27. Radio 2 play more songs you know than Radio 1 - and Jimmy Young has some really interesting guests on…. you know.
28. Instead of tutting at old people who take ages to get off the bus, you tut at schoolchildren whose diction is poor
29. When sitting outside a pub you become envious of their hanging baskets
30. You make an effort to be in and out of the curry house by 11.

31. You come face to face with your own mortality for the first time, and the indestructibility of the 20s gives way to a realisation that you are but passing through this life and if you don't settle down soon and have kids you'll have no- one to look after you when you're old and frail and incontinent and you can't go on p**sing your life up against a wall forever and think of how many brain cells you're destroying every time a swift half turns into 10 pints, and look at that, a full set of stainless steel saucepans for 99 quid, they cost as much as 35 each if you buy them separately, and you get a milk pan thrown in, …
32. You find yourself saying "is it cold in here or is it just me?"

Commerce

Capitalism

TRADITIONAL CAPITALISM
You have two cows
You sell one and buy a bull.
Your herd multiplies, and the economy grows.
You sell them and retire on the income

ENRON VENTURE CAPITALISM
You have two cows. You sell three of them to your publicly listed company, using letters of credit opened by your brother-in-law at the bank, then execute a debt/equity swap with an associated general offer so that you get all four cows back, with a tax exemption for five cows. The milk rights of the six cows are transferred via an intermediary to a Cayman Island company secretly owned by the majority shareholder who sells the rights to all seven cows back to your listed company. The annual report says the company owns eight cows, with an option on one more. The public buys your bull.

A FRENCH CORPORATION

You have two cows. You go on strike because you want three cows.

A JAPANESE CORPORATION

You have two cows. You redesign them so they are one-tenth the size of an ordinary cow and produce twenty times the milk. But instead of selling the milk for consumption, you then create clever cow cartoon images called Cowkimon and market them Worldwide.

A GERMAN CORPORATION

You have two cows. You re-engineer them so they live for 100 years, eat once a month, and milk themselves.

A BRITISH CORPORATION

You have two cows. Both are mad.

AN ITALIAN CORPORATION

You have two cows, but you don't know where they are. You break for lunch.

A RUSSIAN CORPORATION

You have two cows. You count them and learn you have five cows. You count them again and learn you have 42 cows. You count them again and learn you have 12 cows. You stop counting cows and open another bottle of vodka.

A SWISS CORPORATION
You have 5,000 cows, none of which belong to you. You charge others for storing them.

A HINDU CORPORATION
You have two cows. You worship them.

A CHINESE CORPORATION
You have two cows. You have 300 people milking them. You claim full employment, high bovine productivity, and arrest the newsman who reported the numbers.

AN ARKANSAS CORPORATION
You have two cows. That one on the left is kinda cute…

NISSAN
You have two cows. You sell one, and force the other to produce the milk of four cows. You are surprised when the cow drops dead.

Cultural Differences

Party Invitation

He quit his job and bought 50 acres of land in Alaska as far from humanity as possible. He saw the postman once a week and got groceries once a month. Otherwise, it's total peace and quiet.

After six months or so of almost total isolation, someone knocked on his door. He opened it and there is a huge, bearded man standing there.

"Name's Lars, your neighbour from forty miles up the road. Having a Christmas party Friday night ... thought you might like to come ... about 5:00."

"Great," says Tom, "after six months out here I'm ready to meet some local folks. Thank you!"

As Lars is leaving, he stops. "Gotta warn you ... There's gonna be some drink in'."

"Not a problem," says Tom. "After 25 years in business, I can drink with the best of 'em."

Again, as he starts to leave, Lars stops. "More 'n likely gonna be some fightin' too."

Tom says, "Well, I get along with people, I'll be alright. I'll be there. Thanks again."

Once again Lars turns from the door. "More 'n likely be some wild sex, too."

"Now that's really not a problem," says Tom, warming to the idea.

"I've been all alone for six months! I'll definitely be there.

By the way, what should I wear?"

Lars stops in the door again and says,

"Whatever you want. Just gonna be the two of us

Scousers

The Ferrari F1 Team fired their entire Pit-Crew yesterday. The announcement was followed by Ferrari's Decision to take advantage of the English Government's "Work For the Dole" Scheme and hire unemployed youths from Liverpool. The decision to hire them was brought on by a recent documentary on how unemployed youths in Liverpool were able to remove a set of car wheels in less than 6 seconds without proper equipment, whereas Ferrari's existing crew can only do it in 8 seconds.

This was thought to be an excellent yet bold move by Ferrari Management, as most races are won & lost in the pits, Ferrari would have an advantage over every team. However Ferrari expectations were easily exceeded, as during the Crews first practice session; not only were "da boyz from Bootle" able to change the tyres in under 6 seconds but within 12 seconds they had resprayed, rebadged, and had sold the vehicle over to the McLaren Team for four dozen Stella's and a gram of Charlie

Travel Advice

The following advice for American travelers going to France was compiled from information provided by the US State Department, the CIA, the US Chamber of Commerce, the Food and Drug Administration, the Centres for Disease Control and some very expensive spy satellites that the French don't know about. It is intended as a guide for American travelers only.

General Overview

France is a medium-sized foreign country situated in the continent of Europe. It is an important member of the world community, though not nearly as important as it thinks. It is bounded by Germany, Spain, Switzerland and some smaller nations of no particular importance and with not very good shopping.

France is a very old country with many treasures, such as the Louvre and Eurodisney. Among its contributions to western civilization are champagne, Camembert cheese and the guillotine. Although France likes to think of itself as a modern nation, air conditioning is little used and it is next to impossible for Americans to get decent Mexican food. One continuing exasperation for American visitors is that local people insist on speaking in French, though many will speak English if shouted at. Watch your money at all times.

The People

France has a population of 56 million people. 52 million of these drink and smoke (the other 4 million are small children). All French people drive like lunatics, are dangerously oversexed, and have no concept of standing patiently in a queue. The French people are in general gloomy, temperamental, proud, arrogant, aloof and undisciplined; those are their good points. Most French citizens are Roman Catholic, though you would hardly guess it from their behaviour. Many people are communists. Men sometimes have girls' names like Marie or Michel, and they kiss each other when they meet. American travelers are advised to travel in groups and wear baseball caps and colourful trousers for easier recognition.

Safety

In general, France is a safe destination, although travelers must be aware that from time to time it is invaded by Germany. Traditionally, the French surrender immediately and, apart from a temporary shortage of Scotch whisky and increased difficulty in getting baseball scores and stock market prices, life for the American visitor generally goes on much as before. A tunnel connecting France to Britain beneath the English Channel has been opened in recent years to make it easier for the French government to flee to London during future German invasions.

History

France historical figures are Louis XIV, the Huguenots, Joan of Arc, Jacques Cousteau and Charles de Gaulle, who was President for many years and is now an airport.

Government

The French form of government is democratic, but noisy Elections are held more or less continuously and always result in a draw. The French love administration so for government purposes the country is divided into regions, departments, districts, municipalities, towns, communes, villages, cafes, and telephone kiosks. Each of these has its own government and elections. Parliament consists of two chambers, the Upper and Lower, though confusingly they are both on the ground floor, and whose members are either Gaullists or Communists, neither of whom should be trusted by the traveller. Parliament's principal occupation is setting off atomic bombs in the South Pacific and acting indignant and surprised when other countries complain. According to the most current American State Department intelligence, the President is now someone named Jacques. Further information is not available at this time.

Culture

The French pride themselves on their culture, though it is not easy to see why. All their music sounds the same and they have never made a movie that you would want to watch for anything but the nude scenes.

Cuisine

Let's face it, no matter how much garlic you put on it, a snail is just slug with a shell on its back. Croissants on the other hand, are excellent, although it is impossible for most Americans to pronounce this word. In general, travelers are advised to stick to cheeseburgers.

> >

Economy

France has a large and diversified economy, second only to Germany's in Europe, which is surprising because the French hardly work at all. If they are not spending four hours dawdling over lunch, they are on strike and blocking the roads with their trucks and tractors. France's principal exports, in order of importance to the economy, are wine, nuclear weapons, perfume, guided missiles, champagne, guns, grenade launchers, land mines, tanks, attack aircraft, miscellaneous armaments and cheese.

Public Holidays

France has more holidays than any other nation in the world. Among its 361 national holidays are: 197 Saints' days, 37 National Liberation days, 16 Declaration of Republic Days, 54 Return of Charles de Gaulle in triumph as if he won the war single-handed Days, 18 Napoleon sent into Exile Days, 17 Napoleon Called Back from Exile Days, and 2 "France is Great and the rest of the World is Rubbish" Days.

Conclusion

France enjoys a rich history, a picturesque and varied landscape, and a temperate climate. In short, it would be a very nice country if it were not inhabited by French people. The best thing that can be said for France is that it is not Germany.

Boozing can be dangerous

An Englishman, a Dutchman and a Frenchman are all in Saudi Arabia, sharing a smuggled crate of booze when, all of a sudden, Saudi police rush in and arrest them. The mere possession of alcohol is a severe offence in Saudi Arabia, so for the terrible crime of actually being caught consuming the booze, they are all sentenced to death! However, after many months and with the help of very good lawyers, they are able to successfully appeal their sentences down to life imprisonment.

By a stroke of luck, it was a Saudi national holiday the day their trial finished, and the extremely benevolent Sheikh decided they could be released after receiving just 20 lashes each of the whip. As they were preparing for their punishment, the Sheikh announced: "It's my first wife's birthday today, and she has asked me to allow each of you one wish before your whipping." The Dutchman was first in line, he thought for a while and then said: "Please tie a pillow to my back. This was done, but the pillow only lasted 10 lashes before the whip went through. When the punishment was done he had to be carried away bleeding and crying with pain.

The Frenchman was next up. After watching the Dutchman in horror he said smugly: "Please fix two pillows to my back." But even two pillows could only take 15 lashes before the whip went through again and the Frenchman was soon led away whimpering loudly (as they do).

The Englishman was the last one up, but before he could say anything, the Sheikh turned to him and said: "You are from a most beautiful part of the world and your culture is one of the finest in the world. For this, you may have two wishes!"

"Thank you, your Most Royal and Merciful highness", The Englishman replied. "In recognition of your kindness, my first wish is that you give me not 20, but 100 lashes." "Not only are you an honourable, handsome and powerful man, you are also very brave". The Sheikh said with an admiring look on his face. "If 100 lashes is what you desire, then so be it. And your second wish, what is it to be?" the Sheikh asked.

"Tie the Frenchman to my back."

The desert island

Deserted Islands

On a group of beautiful deserted islands in the middle of nowhere,

the following people are stranded:

Two Italian men and one Italian woman

Two French men and one French woman

Two German men and one German woman

Two Greek men and one Greek woman

Two English men and one English woman

Two Irish men and one Irish woman
Two Bulgarian men and one Bulgarian woman
Two Japanese men and one Japanese woman
Two Chinese men and one Chinese woman
Two American men and one American woman

One month later on these absolutely stunning deserted islands in the middle of nowhere, the following things have occurred:

One Italian man killed the other Italian man for the Italian woman.

The two French men and the French woman are living happily together in a menage-a-trois.

The two German men have a strict weekly schedule of alternating visits with the German woman.

The two Greek men are sleeping with each other and the Greek woman is cleaning and cooking for them.

The two English men are waiting for someone to introduce them to the English woman.

The two Irish men divided the island into North and South and set up a distillery. They do not remember if sex is in the picture because it gets sort of foggy after the first few litres of coconut whiskey. But they're satisfied because at least the English aren't having any fun.

The two Bulgarian men took one long look at the endless ocean and another long look at the Bulgarian woman and started swimming.

The two Japanese have faxed Tokyo and are awaiting instructions.

THE GREATEST JOKE COMPENDIUM OF ALL TIME — FOR OUR TIMES

The two Chinese men have set up a pharmacy/liquor store/restaurant/laundry, and have gotten the woman pregnant in order

To supply employees for their store.

The two American men are contemplating the virtues of suicide, because the American woman keeps on complaining about her body, the

True nature of feminism, how she can do everything they can do, the necessity of fulfilment, the equal division of household chores, how sand and palm trees make her look fat, how her last boyfriend respected her opinion and treated her nicer than they do, and how her relationship with her mother is improving, and how at least the taxes are low and it isn't raining.

Chinese proverbs

Virginity like bubble, one prick, all gone.
~~*~*~*~*~*~*~*

Man who run in front of car get tired.
~~*~*~*~*~*~*~*

Man who run behind car get exhausted.
~~*~*~*~*~*~*~*

Man with hand in pocket feel cocky all day.
~~*~*~*~*~*~*~*

Foolish man give wife grand piano, wise man give wife upright organ.
~~*~*~*~*~*~*~*

Man who walk through airport turnstile sideways going to Bangkok.
~~*~*~*~*~*~*~*

Man with one chopstick go hungry.

~~*~*~*~*~*~*~*~*

Man who scratch ass should not bite fingernails.

~~*~*~*~*~*~*~*~*

Man who eat many prunes get good run for money.

* ~*~*~*~*~*~*~*~*~*

Baseball is wrong: man with four balls cannot walk.

~~*~*~*~*~*~*~*~*

Panties not best thing on earth! but next to best thing on earth.

~~*~*~*~*~*~*~*~*

War does not determine who is right, war determine who is left.

~~*~*~*~*~*~*~*~*

Wife who put husband in doghouse soon find him in cat house.

~~*~*~*~*~*~*~*~*

Man who fight with wife all day get no piece at night.

* ~*~*~*~*~*~*~*~*~*

It take many nails to build crib, but one screw to fill it.

~~*~*~*~*~*~*~*~*

Man who drive like hell, bound to get there.

~~*~*~*~*~*~*~*~*

Man who stand on toilet is high on pot.

~~*~*~*~*~*~*~*~*

Man who live in glass house should change clothes in basement.

~~*~*~*~*~*~*~*~*

Man who fish in other man's well often catch crabs.

~~*~*~*~*~*~*~*

Man who fart in church sit in own pew.

~~*~*~*~*~*~*~*

Crowded elevator smell different to midget.

Hospitals in Scotland

An English doctor is being shown around a Scottish hospital. At the e nd of his visit, he's shown into a ward with a number of patients who show no obvious signs of injury. He goes to examine the first man he sees, and the man proclaims:-

"Fair fa' yer honest sonsie face,

Great chieftain o'the puddin' race!

Aboon them a' ye tak your place, painch tripe or thairm:

Weel are ye worthy o' a grace as lang's my arm...."

The doctor, being somewhat taken aback, goes to the next patient, who immediately launches into:-

"Some hae meat, and canna eat,

And some wad eat that want it,

But we hae meat and we can eat,

And sae the Lord be thankit."

This continues with the next patient:-

"Wee sleekit cow'rin tim'rous beastie,

O what a panic's in thy breastie!

Thou need na start awa sae hasty, wi bickering brattle

I wad be laith to run and chase thee, wi murdering prattle!"

"Well," said the Englishman to his Scottish colleague, "I see you saved the psychiatric ward for last."

"No, no, no," the Scottish doctor corrected him, "this is the Serious Burns Unit."

Read the label

In case you needed further proof that the human race is doomed through stupidity, here are some actual label instructions on consumer goods.

On a Sear's hairdryer:
"Do not use while sleeping."
(Gee that's the only time I have to work on my hair.)

On a bag of Fritos:
"You could be a winner! No purchase necessary. Details inside."
(The shoplifter special)

On a bar of Dial soap:
"Directions: Use like regular soap."
(And that would be how …?)

On some Swanson frozen dinners:
"Serving suggestion: Defrost."
(But its "just" a suggestion)

On Tesco's Tiramisu dessert (printed on bottom):
"Do not turn upside down."
(Too late!)

On Marks & Spencer Bread Pudding:
"Product will be hot after heating."
(As night follows day . . .)

On packaging for a Rowenta iron:
"Do not iron clothes on body."
(But wouldn't this save me more time?)

On Boot's Children Cough Medicine:
"Do not drive a car or operate machinery after taking this medication."
(We could do a lot to reduce the rate of construction accidents if we could just get those 5-year-olds with head-colds off those forklifts.)

On Nytol Sleep Aid:
"Warning: May cause drowsiness."
(One would hope.)

On most brands of Christmas lights:
"For indoor or outdoor use only."
(As opposed to what?)

On a Japanese food processor:
"Not to be used for the other use."
(I gotta admit, I'm curious.)

On Sainsbury's peanuts:
"Warning: contains nuts."
(Talk about a news flash.)

On an American Airlines packet of nuts:
"Instructions: Open packet, eat nuts."
(Step 3: Fly Delta.)

On a child's superman costume:
"Wearing of this garment does not enable you to fly."
(I don't blame the company. I blame parents for this one.)

On a Swedish chainsaw:
"Do not attempt to stop chain with your hands or genitals."
(Was there a lot of this happening somewhere? My God!)

Drinking buddies

An Englishman, Aussie and South African were sitting in a bar one night having a beer. All of a sudden the South African drinks his beer, throws his glass in the air, pulls out a gun shoots the glass to pieces and says "In Sath Afrika our glasses are so cheap that we don't need to drink from the same one twice".

The Aussie obviously impressed by this (simple things….) drinks his beer, throws his glass into the air, pulls out his gun and shoots the glass to pieces and says "Well mate, in 'straaaaailia we have so much sand to make the glasses that we don't need to drink out of the same glass twice either".

The Englishman, cool as a cucumber, picks up his beer and drinks it, throws his glass into the air, pulls out his gun and shoots the South African and the Australian and says "In England we have so many fucking South Africans and Australians that we don't need to drink with the same ones twice".

Top 10 reasons for your nationality

TOP 10 REASONS FOR BEING FRENCH:
1. When speaking fast you can make yourself sound intelligent
2. Own half the world's perfume industry and still never use deodorant
3. You get to eat insect food like snails and frog's legs
4. If there's a war you can surrender really early
5. You don't have to read the subtitles on late night films on Channel 4
6. You can test your own nuclear weapons in other people's countries
7. You can be ugly and still become a famous film star
8. Allow Germans to march up and down your most famous street humiliating your sense of national pride
9. You don't have to bother with toilets, just shit in the street
10. People think you're a great lover even when you're not

TOP 10 REASONS FOR BEING AMERICAN:
1. You can have a woman president without electing her
2. You can spell colour wrong and get away with it
3. You can call Budweiser beer
4. You can be a crook/adulterer and still be president
5. If you've got enough money you can get elected to do anything
6. If you can breathe you can get a gun
7. You can invent a new public holiday every year
8. You can play golf in the most hideous clothes ever made and nobody seems to care
9. You get to call everyone you've never met "buddy"
10. You can think you're the greatest nation on earth for no reason at all

TOP 10 REASONS FOR BEING ENGLISH:
1. Two World Wars and One World Cup doo-dah doo-dah
2. Warm beer
3. You get to confuse everyone with the rules of cricket
4. You get to accept defeat graciously in major sporting events
5. Union jack underpants

6. Water shortages guaranteed every single summer
7. You can live in the past and imagine you are still a world power
8. Fish and chips
9. Beats being Welsh
10. Or Scottish

TOP 10 REASONS FOR BEING ITALIAN:

1. In-depth knowledge of bizarre pasta shapes
2. Unembarrassed to wear fur
3. No need to worry about tax returns
4. Glorious military history… well, till about 400 AD
5. Can wear sunglasses inside
6. Political stability
7. Flexible working hours
8. Live near the Pope
9. Can spend hours braiding girlfriend's armpit hair
10. Country run by Sicilian murderers

TOP 10 REASONS FOR BEING SPANISH:

1. Glorious history of killing South American tribes
2. The rest of Europe thinks Africa begins at the Pyrenees
3. You get your beaches invaded by Germans, Danes, Brits etc

4. The rest of your country is already invaded by Moroccans
5. Everybody else makes crap paella and claims it's the real thing
6. Honesty
7. Only sure way of bedding a woman is to dress up in stupid, tight clothes and risk your life in front of bulls
8. You get to eat bulls' testicles
9. Gibraltar
10. Supported Argentina in Falklands War

TOP 10 REASONS FOR BEING GERMAN:

1.
2.
3.
4.
5.
6.
7.
8.
9.
10.

TOP 10 REASONS FOR BEING INDIAN:

1. Chicken Madras
2. Lamb Passanda
3. Onion Bhaji
4. Bombay Potato

5. Chicken Tikka Masala
6. Rogan Josh
7. Popadoms
8. Chicken Dopiaza
9. Meat Bhuna
10. Kingfisher lager

TOP 10 REASONS FOR BEING WELSH:
1 to 10. Sheep

TOP 10 REASONS FOR BEING IRISH:
1. Guinness
2. 18 children because you can't use contraceptives
3. You can get into a fight just by marching down someone's road
4. Pubs never close
5. Can use Papal edicts on contraception passed in the second Vatican Council of 1968 to persuade your girlfriend that you can't have sex with a condom on
6. No one can ever remembers the night before
7. Kill people you don't agree with
8. Stew
9. More Guinness
10. Eating stew and drinking Guinness in an Irish pub at 3 in the morning after a bout of sectarian violence

TOP 10 REASONS FOR BEING CANADIAN:
1. It beats being an American

2. Only country to successfully invade the US and burn its capital to the ground
3. You can play hockey 12 months a year, outdoors
4. Only country to successfully invade the US and burn its capital to the ground
5. Where else can you travel 1000 miles over fresh water in a canoe?
6. A political leader can admit to smoking pot and his/her popularity ratings will rise
7. Only country to successfully invade the US and burn its capital to the ground
8. Kill Grizzly bears with huge shotguns and cover your house in their skins
9. Own-an-Eskimo scheme
10. Only country to successfully invade the US and burn its capital to the ground

TOP 10 REASONS FOR BEING AUSTRALIAN:

1. Know your great-grand-dad was a murdering bastard that no civilised nation on earth wanted (i.e.: You get to live in what was Britain's largest "open prison")
2. Fosters Lager
3. Dispossess Aborigines who have lived in your country for 40,000 years because you think it belongs to you
4. Annihilate England every time you play them at cricket
5. Tact and sensitivity

6. Bondi Beach
7. Other beaches
8. Liberated attitude to homosexuals
9. Drinking cold lager on the beach
10. Having a bit of a swim and then drink some cold lager on the beach

TOP 10 REASONS FOR BEING A KIWI:

1. Get to shag chicks that resemble Jonah Lomu in a frock
2. Beer
3. Rugby
4. See above
5. See above
6. See above
7. See above
8. See above
9. You can tap a girl on her head and her knickers fall down
10. Hate everyone else ……unless its their round

Nelson Mandela

Nelson Mandela is sitting at home watching the telly when he hears a knock at the door. When he opens it, he is confronted by a little Chinese man, clutching a clipboard and yelling, "You sign! You sign!" Behind him is an enormous truck full of car exhausts. Nelson is standing there in complete amazement, when the Chinese man starts to yell louder.

"You sign! You sign!"

Nelson says to him, "Look mate, you've obviously got the wrong guy. Push off" and shuts the door in his face. The next day he hears a knock at the door again. When he opens it, the little Chinese man is back with a huge truck of brake pads. He thrusts his clipboard under Nelson's nose, yelling, "You sign! You sign!" Mandela is getting a bit hacked off by now, so he shoves the little Chinese man back, shouting: "Look, push off! You've got the wrong bloke! I don't want them!" Then he slams the door in his face again.

The following day, Nelson is resting and late in the afternoon he hears a knock on the door again. On opening the door, there is the same little Chinese man thrusting a clipboard under his nose, shouting "You sign! You sign!" Behind him are TWO very large trucks full of car parts. This time Nelson loses his temper completely, he picks up the little man by his shirtfront and yells at him; "Look, I don't want these! Do you understand? You must have the wrong name! Who do you want to give these to?"

The little Chinese man looks at him very puzzled, consults his clipboard, and says:

"You not Nissan Maindealer?"

Questions of Ethics

Your choice

You are driving along in your car on a wild, stormy night. You pass by a bus stop, and you see three people waiting for the bus:
1. An old lady who looks as if she is about to die.
2. An old friend who once saved your life.
3. The perfect man (or) woman you have been dreaming about.

There can only be one passenger in your car and you can't return to the bus stop once you have left it (I don't know why, it's just part of this question!). Which one would you choose to offer a ride?

Think before you continue reading. This is a moral/ethical dilemma that was once actually used as part of a job selection process.

You could pick up the old lady, because she is going to die, and thus you should save her first; or you could take the old friend because he once saved your life, and this would be the perfect chance to pay him back.

However, you may never be able to find your perfect dream lover again. The candidate who was hired (out of 200 applicants) had no trouble coming up with his answer.

WHAT DID HE SAY? (Scroll down)

He answered: "I would give the car keys to my old friend, and let him take the old lady to the hospital. I would stay behind and wait for the bus with the woman of my dreams."

The moral of the story — "Think Outside of the Box."

Celebs

Big Sean

Sean Connery was interviewed by Michael Parkinson, and bragged that despite his 72 years of age, he could still have sex three times a night. Lulu, who was also a guest, looked intrigued.

After the show, Lulu said, "Sean, if Ah'm no bein too forward, Ah'd love tae hae sex wi an aulder man. Let's go back tae mah place." So they go back to her place and have great sex.

Afterwards, Sean says, "If you think that was good, let me shleep for half an hour, and we can have even better shex. But while I'm shleeping, hold my baws in your left hand and my wullie in your right hand." Lulu looks a bit perplexed, but says, "Okay." He sleeps for half an hour, awakens, and they have even better sex.

Then Sean says, "Lulu, that was wonderful. But if you let me shleep for an hour, we can have the besht shex yet. But again, hold my baws in your left hand, and my wullie in your right hand." Lulu is now used to the routine and complies. The results are mind blowing.

Once it's all over, and the cigarettes are lit, Lulu asks "Sean, tell me, diz mah haudin' yer baws in mah left hand and yer wullie in mah right stimulate ye while ye're sleepin?"

Sean replies, "No, but the lasht time I shlept with a Glashwegian, she shtole my wallet."

Sherlock Holmes

Sherlock Holmes and Mr. Watson went on a camping trip.

After a good meal and a bottle of wine they lay down in their tent for the night and went to sleep. Some hours later, Holmes awoke and nudged his faithful friend awake.

"Watson, look up at the sky and tell me what you see."

Watson replied, "I see millions and millions of stars."

"What does that tell you?" Holmes questioned.

Watson pondered for a minute. "Astronomically, it tells me that there are billions of galaxies and potentially billions of planets.

Astrologically, I observe Saturn is in Leo.

Logically, I deduce that the time is approximately a quarter past three.

Theologically, I can see that God is all-powerful and that we are

small and insignificant.

Meteorologically, I suspect that we will have a beautiful day tomorrow".

"Is that all?" Holmes asked.

"Yes." Watson replied. "Why, am I missing something?"

Holmes was quiet for a moment, and then spoke:

"Watson, you dickhead. Someone has stolen the fucking tent."

Philosophy

Cats

1. Cats do what they want, when they want.
2. They rarely listen to you.
3. They're totally unpredictable.
4. They whine when they are unhappy.
5. When you want to play, they want to be left alone.
6. When you want to be alone, they want to play.
7. They expect you to cater for their every whim.
8. They're moody.
9. They leave their hair everywhere.
10. They drive you nuts!

CONCLUSION: Cats are small women in fur coats>

Dogs

1. Dogs lie around all day, sprawled on the most comfortable piece of furniture in the house.

2. They can hear a package of food being opened two streets away, but don't hear you when you're in the same room.
3. They can look dumb and lovable at the same time.
4. They growl when they are unhappy.
5. When you want to play, they want to play.
6. When you want to be left alone, they want to play.
7. They are great at begging.
8. They will love you forever if you rub their tummies.
9. They leave their toys everywhere.
10. They do disgusting things with their mouths and then try to give you a kiss.

CONCLUSION: Dogs are small men in fur coats!!

Why did the chicken cross the road?

PAT BUCHANAN:

To steal a job from a decent, hardworking American.

DR. SEUSS:

Did the chicken cross the road? Did he cross it with a toad?

Yes! The chicken crossed the road, but why it crossed, I've not been told!

ERNEST HEMINGWAY:
To die. In the rain.

MARTIN LUTHER KING, JR.:
I envision a world where all chickens will be free to cross roads without having their motives called into question.

GRANDPA:
In my day, we didn't ask why the chicken crossed the road. Someone told us the chicken crossed the road, and that was good enough for us.

ARISTOTLE:
It is the nature of chickens to cross the road.

KARL MARX:
It was a historical inevitability.

SADDAM HUSSEIN:
This was an unprovoked act of rebellion and we were quite justified in dropping 50 tons of nerve gas on it.

CAPTAIN JAMES T. KIRK:
To boldly go where no chicken has gone before.

FREUD:
The fact that you are at all concerned that the chicken crossed the road reveals your underlying sexual insecurity.

BILL GATES:
I have just released eChicken 98, which will not only cross roads, but will lay eggs, file your important documents, and balance your checkbook - and Internet Explorer is an inextricable part of the Chicken.

EINSTEIN:
Did the chicken really cross the road or did the road move beneath the chicken?

BILL CLINTON:
I did not cross the road with THAT chicken. What do you mean by chicken? Could you define chicken please?

LOUIS FARRAKHAN:
The road, you will see, represents the black man. The chicken crossed the "black man" in order to trample him and keep him down.

THE BIBLE:
And God came down from the heavens, and He said unto the chicken,
"Thou shalt cross the road." And the chicken crossed the road, and there was much rejoicing.

COLONEL SANDERS:
I missed one?

Bill G

An unemployed man went to apply for a job with Microsoft as a janitor. The manager there arranges for him to take an aptitude test. After the test, the manager says, "You will be employed as a janitor at minimum wage, $5.15 an hour. Let me have your e-mail address, so that I can send you a form to complete and tell you where to report for work on your first day."

Taken aback, the man protests that he has neither a computer nor an e-mail address. To this the MS manager replies, "Well, then, that means that you virtually don't exist and can therefore hardly expect to be employed by Microsoft. Stunned, the man leaves. Not knowing where to turn and having only $10.00 in his wallet, he buys a 25 lb flat of tomatoes at the supermarket.

In less two hours, he sells all the tomatoes individually at 100% profit. Repeating the process several times more that day, he ends up with almost $100.00 before going to sleep that night.

Thus it dawns on him that he could quite easily make a living selling tomatoes.

Getting up early every day and going to bed late, he multiplies profits quickly. After a short time he acquires a cart to transport several dozen boxes of tomatoes, only to have to trade it in again so that he can buy a pickup truck to support his expanding business. By the end of the second year, he is the owner of a fleet of pickup trucks and manages a staff of a hundred former unemployed people, all selling tomatoes.

Planning for the future of his wife and children, he decides to buy some life insurance. Consulting with an insurance adviser, he picks an insurance plan to fit his new circumstances. At the end of the telephone conversation, the adviser asks him for his e-mail address in order to send the final documents electronically. When the man replies that he has no e-mail, the adviser is stunned. "What, you don't have e-mail? How on earth have you managed to amass such wealth without the Internet, e-mail and e-commerce? Just imagine where you would be now, if you had been connected to the Internet from the very start!" "Well," replied the tomato millionaire, "I would be a janitor at Microsoft!"

By definition, a fable must have a moral. This one has four:
1. The Internet, e-mail and e-commerce do not need to rule your life.
2. If you don't have e-mail, but work hard, you can still become millionaire.
3. Since you got this story via e-mail, you're probably closer to becoming a janitor than you are to becoming a millionaire.
4. If you do have a computer and e-mail, you have already been taken to the cleaners by Microsoft.

Musings

If quizzes are quizzical, what are tests?

If electricity comes from electrons, does morality come from morons?

Why do toasters always have a setting so high that could burn the toast to a horrible crisp, which no decent human being would eat?

Why is there a light in the fridge and not in the freezer?

Why do people point to their wrist when asking for the time, but don't point to their bum when they ask where the bathroom is?

Why does Goofy stand erect while Pluto remains on all fours? They're both dogs!

If corn oil is made from corn, and vegetable oil is made from vegetables, then what is baby oil made from?

Is Disney World the only people trap operated by a mouse?

Why do the Alphabet song and Twinkle, Twinkle Little Star have the same tune?

Stop singing and read on . . . .

Why do they call it an asteroid when it's outside the hemisphere, but call it a haemorrhoid when it's on the outside of your bum?

Did you ever notice that when you blow in a dog's face, he gets mad at you, but when you take him on a car ride, he sticks his head out the window?

Who was the first person to look at a cow and say, "I think I'll
squeeze these pink dangly things here and drink whatever comes out?"

Who was the first person to say, "See that chicken there… I'm going to eat the next thing that comes outta its bum."

The boy learns!

A young boy went up to his father and asked, what is the difference between potentially and realistically?? The father pondered for a while, then answered, "Go ask your mother if she would sleep with Robert Redford for a million dollars. Also, ask your sister if she would sleep with Brad Pitt for a million dollars. Come back and tell me what you have learned".

So the boy went to his mother and asked, "Would you sleep with
Robert Redford for a million dollars?" The mother replied, "Of course I would. I wouldn't pass up an opportunity like that".

The boy then went to his sister and said, "Would you sleep with Brad Pitt for a million dollars?"The girl replied, "Oh gosh!! I would just love to do that! I would be nuts to pass up that opportunity!"

The boy then thought about it for two or three days and went back
to his dad. His father asked him, "Did you find out the difference
between potential and realistic?" The boy replied, "Yes, potentially we're sitting on two million dollars, but realistically we're living with two slappers".

The father replied: "That's my boy!"

A model for life's meaning.

A philosophy professor stood before his class and had some items in front of him. When the class began, wordlessly he picked up a large empty mayonnaise jar and proceeded to fill it with rocks, rocks about 2" in diameter. He then asked the students if the jar was full? They agreed that it was.

So the professor then picked up a box of pebbles and poured them into the jar. He shook the jar lightly. The pebbles, of course, rolled into the open areas between the rocks. He then asked the students again if the jar was full. They agreed it was.

The students laughed. The professor picked up a box of sand and poured it into the jar. Of course, the sand filled up everything else. "Now," said the professor, "I want you to recognise that this is your life. The rocks are the important things - your family, your partner, your health, and your children - things that if everything else was lost and only they remained, your life would still be full.

The pebbles are the other things that matter like your job, your house, and your car. The sand is everything else. The small stuff." "If you put the sand into the jar first, there is no room for the pebbles or the rocks.

The same goes for your life. If you spend all your time and energy on the seer.

Terror

Warning

I received this today and the warning is genuine.

Yesterday, a friend was travelling on a Paris to London flight.

A man of Arabic appearance got off the plane and my friend noticed that he had left his bag behind.

She grabbed the bag and ran after him, caught up with him in the terminal and handed him back his bag. He was extremely grateful and reached into his bag which appeared to contain large bundles of money.

He looked around to make sure nobody was looking and whispered "I can never repay your kindness, but I will try to….with a word of advice for you: Stay away from Wales".

My friend was genuinely terrified. "Is there going to be an attack?" she asked him.

No … ", he whispered back…… "It's a shit-hole."

This boy will go far

Little David comes home from first grade and tells his father that they learned about the history of Valentine's Day. "Since Valentine's Day is for a Christian saint and we're Jewish," he asks, "will God get mad at me for giving someone a > >valentine?" David's father thinks a bit, then says, "No, I don't think God would get mad. Who do you want to give a valentine to?" "Osama Bin Laden," David says.

"Why Osama Bin Laden?" his father asks in shock.

"Well," David says, "I thought that if a little American Jewish boy could have enough love to give Osama a valentine, he might start to think that maybe we're not all bad, and maybe start loving people a little bit. And if other kids saw what I did and sent valentines to Osama, he'd love everyone a lot. And then he'd start going all over the place to tell everyone how much he loved them and how he didn't hate anyone anymore."

His father's heart swells and he looks at his boy with newfound pride. "David, that's the most wonderful thing I've ever heard." "I know," David says, "and once that gets him out in the open, the Marines could blow the shit out of him."

Religion

Three Pastors from the south were having lunch in a diner. One said, "Ya know, since summer started I've been having trouble with bats in my loft and attic at church. I've tried everything-noise, spray, cats-nothing seems to scare them away.

Another said, "Yea, me too. I've got hundreds living in my belfry and in the attic. I've even had the place fumigated, and they won't go away."

The third said, "I baptized all mine, and made them members of the church… Haven't seen one back since!"

Appearances can be deceptive!

A nun who works for a local home health care agency was out making her rounds when she ran out of gas. As luck would have it there was a station just down the street. She walked to the station to borrow a can with enough gas to start the car and drive to the station for a fill up.

The attendant regretfully told her that the only can he owned had just been loaned out, but if she would care to wait he was sure it would be back shortly. Since the nun was on the way to see a patient she decided not to wait and walked back to her car.

After looking through her car for something to carry to the station to fill with gas, she spotted a bedpan she was taking to the patient. Always resourceful, she carried it to the station and filled it with gasoline. As she was pouring the gas into the tank of her car two men walked by. One was heard to exclaim, "Now that is what I call faith!"

Spread a little happiness

The other day I went into the local religious book store, where I saw a "Honk if you love Jesus" bumper sticker. I bought it and put it on the back bumper of my car, and I'm really glad I did. What an uplifting experience followed!

I was stopped at a light at a busy intersection, just lost in thoughts of the Lord, and I didn't notice that the light had changed. That bumper sticker really worked! I found lots of people who loved Jesus. Why, the guy behind me started to honk like crazy. He must really love the Lord because pretty soon, he leaned out his window and yelled "Jesus Christ" as loud as he could. It was like a football game, with his shouting, "Go Jesus Christ Go."

Everyone else started honking, too, so I leaned out my window and waved and smiled to all those loving people. There must have been a guy from Florida back there because I could hear him yelling something about a "sunny beach", and I saw him waving in a funny way with his middle finger stuck up in the air. I asked my two kids what that meant, they squirmed, looked at each other, giggled and told me that it was the Hawaiian good luck sign, so I leaned out the window and gave him the good luck sign back.

Several cars behind, a very nice large man stepped out of his car and yelled something. I couldn't hear him very well, but it sounded like "mother trucker" or mother from there. Maybe he was from Florida too. He must really love the Lord.

A couple of the people were so caught up in the joy of the moment that they got out of their cars and were walking toward me. I bet they wanted to pray, but just then I noticed the light had changed to yellow, and I stepped on the gas. And a good thing I did, because I was the only driver to get across the intersection. I looked back at them standing there. I leaned way out the window, gave them a big smile and held up the Hawaiian good luck sign and I drove away.

Praise the Lord for such wonderful people!

The bible says……

A young boy had just gotten his driving permit. He asked his father, who was a minister, if they could discuss the use of the car. His father took him to his study and said to him, "I'll make a deal with you. You bring your grades up, study your Bible a little and get your hair cut and we'll talk about it."

After about a month the boy came back and again asked his father if they could discuss use of the car. They again went to the father's study where his father said, "Son, I've been real proud of you. You have brought your grades up, you've studied your Bible diligently, but you didn't get your hair cut!"

The young man waited a moment and replied, "You know Dad, I've been thinking about that. You know, Samson had long hair, Moses had long hair, Noah had long hair, and even Jesus had long hair...."

To which his father replied, "Yes, and they walked everywhere they went!"

B I G Trouble

In a certain suburban neighbourhood, there were two brothers, 8 and 10 years old, who were exceedingly mischievous. Whenever something went wrong in the neighbourhood, it turned out they had a hand in it. Their parents were at their wits' end trying to control them. Hearing about a minister nearby who worked with delinquent boys, the mother suggested to the father that they ask the minister to talk with the boys. The father agreed.

The mother went to the minister and made her request. He agreed, but said he wanted to see the younger boy first and alone. So the mother sent him to the minister. The minister sat the boy down on the other side of his huge, impressive desk. For about five minutes they just sat and stared at each other.

Finally, the minister pointed his forefinger at the boy and asked, "Where is God?"

The boy looked under the desk, in the corners of the room, all around, but said nothing. Again, louder, the minister pointed at the boy and asked, "Where is God?"

Again the boy looked all around but said nothing.

A third time, in a louder, firmer voice, the minister leaned far across the desk and put his forefinger almost to the boy's nose, and asked, "Where is God?"

The boy panicked and ran all the way home. Finding his older brother, he dragged him upstairs to their room and into the closet, where they usually plotted their mischief. He finally said, "We are in B-I-I-I-G trouble now!"

The older boy asked, "What do you mean, B-I-I-I-G trouble?"

His brother replied, "God is missing and they think we did it."

Ingenuity!

A little nine year old girl was in church with her mother when she started feeling ill. "Mommy," she said. "Can we leave now?"

"No," her mother replied.

"Well, I think I have to throw up!"

"Then go out the front door and around to the back of the church and throw up behind a bush." In about two minutes the little girl returned to her seat.

"Did you throw up?" her mother asked.

"Yes," the little girl replied.

"Well, how could you have gone all the way to the back of the church and return so quickly?"

"I didn't have to go out of the church, Mommy." the little girl replied. "They have a box next to the front door that says, 'For the sick'."

Forrest Gump – now he's sharp!

The day finally arrived: Forest Gump dies and goes to Heaven. St. Peter himself meets him at the Pearly Gates. The gates are closed, however, and Forest approaches the gatekeeper.

Saint Peter says, "Well, Forest, it's certainly good to see you. We have heard a lot about you. I must inform you that the place is filling up fast, and we've been administering an entrance examination for everyone. The tests are fairly short, but you need to pass before you can get into Heaven."

Forest responds, "It shore is good to be here St. Peter. I was looking forward to this. Nobody ever told me about any entrance exams. Sure hope the test ain't too hard; life was a big enough test as it was."

St. Peter goes on, "Yes, I know Forest. But the test I have for you is only three questions. Here is the first: What days of the week begin with the letter 'T'? Second, how many seconds are there in a year? Third, what is God's first name?"

Forest goes away to think the questions over. He returns the next day and goes up to St. Peter to try to answer the exam questions.

St. Peter waves him up and asks, "Now that you have had a chance to think the questions over, tell me your answers."

Forest says, "Well, the first one, how many days of the week begin with the letter 'T'? Shucks, that one's easy; that'd be Today and Tomorrow!"

The saint's eyes open wide and he exclaims, "Forest! That's not what I was thinking, but …you do have a point though, and I guess I didn't specify, so I give you credit for that answer."

"How about the next one," says St. Peter, "How many seconds in a year?"

"Now that one's harder," says Forest. "But, I thunk and thunk about that, and I guess the only answer can be twelve."

Astounded, St. Peter says, "Twelve! Twelve! Forest, how in Heaven's name could you come up with twelve seconds in a year?"

Forest says, "Shucks, there gotta be twelve: January second, February second, March second….."

"Hold it," interrupts St., Peter. "I see where you're going with it. And I guess I see your point, though that wasn't quite what I had in mind, but I'll give you credit for that one too."

"Let's go on with the next and final question," says St. Peter, "Can you tell me God's first name?"

Forest says, "Well shore, I know God's first name. Everbody probly knows it. It's Howard."

"Howard?" asks St. Peter. "What makes you think it's 'Howard'?"

Forest answers, "It's in the prayer."

"The prayer?" asks St. Peter, "Which prayer?"

"The Lord's Prayer," responds Forest: "Our Father, who art in heaven, Howard be thy name…."

An audience with the Pope

A gentleman had been trying for years to meet the Pope. Finally, his wish was granted. When the gentleman approached the Pope he said, "Your Eminence, I am so happy to be given this chance to speak with you and I would like to tell you a joke before I start."

The Pope replied, "Of course my son. Go ahead and tell your joke."

The gentleman continued, "There were these two Pollacks and…"

The Pope interrupted, "My son, do you realize that I am Polish?"

"I'm sorry, your Eminence. I'll speak slower."

Be careful what you wish for

A local preacher was dissatisfied with the small amount in the collection plates each Sunday. Someone suggested to him that perhaps he might be able to hypnotize the congregation into giving more. "And just how would I go about doing that?" he asked.

"It is very simple. First you turn up the air conditioner so that the auditorium is warmer than usual. Then you preach in a monotone. Meanwhile, you dangle a watch on a chain and swing it in a slow arc above the lectern and suggest they put 20 dollars in the collection plate."

So the very next Sunday, the reverend did as suggested, and lo and behold the plates were full of 20 dollar bills.

Now, the preacher did not want to take advantage of this technique each and every Sunday. So therefore, he waited for a couple of weeks and then tried his mass hypnosis again. Just as the last of the congregation was becoming mesmerized, the chain on the watch broke and the watch hit the lectern with a loud thud and springs and parts flew everywhere.

"Crap!" exclaimed the pastor.

It took them a week to clean up the church.

They really wrote these

These are actual clippings from church newspapers.

It's amazing what a little proof reading could've prevented:

Bertha Belch, a missionary from Africa will be speaking tonight at The

Calvary Memorial Church in Racine.

Come tonight and hear Bertha Belch all the way from Africa.

Don't forget the National PRAYER & FASTING Conference. "The cost for

attending the Fasting and Prayer conference includes meals."

Miss Charlene Mason sang, "I Will Not Pass This Way Again," giving

obvious pleasure to the congregation.

"Ladies, don't forget the rummage sale. It's a chance to get rid ofthose things not worth keeping around the house.

Don't forget your husbands."

The peacemaking meeting scheduled for today has been cancelled due to a conflict.

The sermon this morning: "Jesus Walks on the Water"

The sermon tonight will be: "Searching for Jesus"

Barbara Jones remains in the hospital and needs blood donors for more transfusions. She is also having trouble sleeping and requests tapes of Reverend Jackson's sermons.

The Rector will preach his farewell message after which the choir will sing "Break Forth into Joy."

Don't let worry kill you - let the Church help.

Irving Benson and Jessica Carter were married on October 24 in the church. So ends a friendship that began in their school days.

At the evening service tonight, the sermon topic will be "What is Hell?" Come early and listen to our choir practice.

Eight new choir robes are currently needed, due to the addition of several new members and to the deterioration of some older ones.

The senior choir invites any member of the congregation who enjoy sinning to join the choir.

Scouts are saving aluminium cans, bottles, and other items to be recycled.
Proceeds will be used to cripple children.

For those of you who have children and don't know it, we have a nursery downstairs.

Potluck supper Sunday at 5:00 P.M.-prayer and medication to follow.

The ladies of the Church have cast off clothing of every kind. They may be seen in the basement on Friday afternoon.

This evening at 7 P.M. there will be a hymn sing in the park across from the Church. Bring a blanket and come prepared to sin.

The pastor would appreciate it if the ladies of the congregation would lend him their electric girdles for the pancake breakfast next Sunday morning.

Low Self Esteem Support Group will meet Thursday at 8 PM, Please use the back door.

Weight Watchers will meet at 7 PM at the First Presbyterian Church.

Please use the large double door at the side.

Adam

As you all know, in the Beginning, God created Heaven and Earth and then He created man:

God said, "Adam, I want you to do something for me."

Adam said, "Gladly, Lord, what do you want me to do?"

God said, "Go down into that valley."

Adam said, "What's a valley?"

God explained it to him.

Then God said, "Cross the river."

Adam said, "What's a river?"

God explained that to him, and then said,

"Go over to the hill……."

Adam said, "What is a hill?"

So, God explained to Adam what a hill was. He told Adam, "On the other side of the hill you will find a cave" Adam said, "What's a cave?" After God explained, he said, "In the cave you will find a Woman." Adam said, "What's a woman?" So God explained that to him, too. Then, God said, "I want you to go forth and reproduce." Adam said, "How do I do that?" God first said (under his breath), "Geez….." And then, just like everything else, God explained that to Adam, as well. So, Adam goes down into the valley, across the river, and over the hill, into the cave, and finds the woman.

In about five minutes, he was back. God, his patience wearing thin, said angrily, "What is it now?"

And Adam said, "What's a headache?"

Jesus - Jewish, Italian, Irish or?

There are 3 good arguments that Jesus was Black:
1. He called everyone "brother".
2. He liked Gospel.
3. He couldn't get a fair trial.

But then there are 3 equally good arguments that Jesus was Jewish:
1. He went into His Father's business.
2. He lived at home until he was 33.
3. He was sure his Mother was a virgin and his mother was sure he was God.

But then there were 3 equally good arguments that Jesus was Italian:
1. He talked with his hands.
2. He had wine with every meal.
3. He used olive oil.

But then there were 3 equally good arguments that Jesus was a Californian:
1. He never cut his hair.
2. He walked around barefoot all the time.
3. He started a new religion.

Yet there were 3 equally good arguments that Jesus was Irish:
1. He never got married.
2. He was always telling stories.
3. He loved green pastures.

But the most compelling evidence of all - 3 proofs that Jesus was a Woman:

1. He had to feed a crowd at a moment's notice when there was no food.
2. He kept trying to get a message across to a bunch of men who just didn't get it.
3. Even when He was dead, He had to get up because there was more work for him to do.

Brainteasers

Fs

Count the number of "F's" in the following text:
FINISHED FILES ARE THE RESULT OF YEARS OF SCIENTIFIC STUDY COMBINED WITH THE EXPERIENCE OF YEARS

Finished? Scroll down only after you have counted them, okay?

How many? 3?

Wrong, there are 6!! —No joke! Read it again.

The reasoning behind is further down

The brain cannot process "OF".

Incredible or what?

Anyone who counts all 6 "F's" on the first go is a genius. Three is normal, four is quite rare.

Modern Living

You know you are living in the current age when:

1. You accidentally enter your password on the microwave.
2. You haven't played solitaire with real cards in years.
3. You have a list of 15 phone numbers to reach your family of 3.
4. You e-mail your friend who works at the desk next to you.
5. Your reason for not staying in touch with friends is that they do not have e-mail addresses.
6. When you go home after a long day at work you still answer the phone in a business manner
7. When you make phone calls from home, you accidentally dial "9" to get an outside line.
8. You've sat at the same desk for four years and worked for three
9. different companies.
10. You learn about your lay-off on the 10 o'clock news.

11. Your boss doesn't have the ability to do your job.
12. Contractors outnumber permanent staff and are more likely to get long-service awards.

.. and the real clinchers are…

13. You read this entire list, and kept nodding and smiling.
14. As you read this list, you think about forwarding it to your "friends".
15. You got this e-mail from a friend that never talks to you any more, except to send you jokes from the net.
16. You are too busy to notice there was no # 9.
17. You actually scrolled back up to check that there wasn't a No.9.

Boy is he miserable

Things I hate about everybody

1. People who point at their wrist while asking for the time…. I know where my watch is pal, where the f*ck is yours? Do I point at my crotch when I ask where the toilet is?
2. People who are willing to get off their arse to search the entire room for the TV remote because they refuse to walk to the TV and change the channel manually.
3. When people say, "Oh you just want to have your cake and eat it too". Fucking right! What good is a cake if you can't eat it?
4. When people say "it's always the last place you look". Of course it is. Why the f*ck would you

keep looking after you've found it? Do people do this? Who and where are they?

5. When people say while watching a film "did you see that?". No tosser, I paid 10 quid to come to the cinema and stare at the fucking floor.

6. People who ask, "Can I ask you a question?". Didn't really give me a choice there, did you sunshine?

7. When something is 'new and improved!'. Which is it? If it's new, then there has never been anything before it. If it's an improvement, then there must have been something before it.

8. When people say, "life is short". What the f*ck?? Life is the longest damn thing anyone ever fucking does!! What can you do that's longer?

9. When you are waiting for the bus and someone asks, "Has the bus come yet?" If the bus came would I be standing here, Knobhead?

10. People who say things like 'My eyes aren't what they used to be'. So what did they used to be? ears, Wellington boots?

11. When you're eating something and someone asks 'Is that nice?' No it's really revolting - I always eat stuff I hate.

12. People who announce they are going to the toilet. Thanks that's an image I really didn't need.

13. McDonalds staff who pretend they don't understand you unless you insert the 'Mc' before the item you are ordering….. It's has

to be a McChicken Burger, just a Chicken Burger get blank looks……….. Well I'll have a McStraw and jam it in your McEyes you fucking McTosser.
14. When you're involved in a accident and someone asks 'are you alright? Yes fine thanks, I'll just pick up my limbs and be off.

How's your relationship with the bank?

The following is a letter received by a major US bank recently - and yes, it's for real It was printed by the New York Times!

Dear Bank Manager,

I am writing to thank you for bouncing the cheque with which I endeavored to pay my plumber last month. By my calculations some three nanoseconds must have elapsed between his presenting the cheque, and the arrival in my account of the funds needed to honour it. I refer, of course, to the automatic monthly deposit of my entire salary, an arrangement that, I admit, has only been in place for eight years.

You are to be commended for seizing that brief window of opportunity, for debiting my account with $50 by way of penalty, and for the way this incident has caused me to re-think my errant financial ways.

You have set me on the path of fiscal righteousness. No more will our relationship be blighted by these unpleasant incidents, for I am restructuring my affairs in 1999, taking as my model the procedures, attitudes and conduct of your very own bank. I can think of no greater compliment, and I know you will be excited and proud to hear it.

To this end, please be advised about the following changes.

First, I have noticed that whereas I personally attend to your telephone calls and letters, when I try to contact you I am confronted by the impersonal, ever-changing, pre-recorded, faceless entity, which your bank has become.

From now on I, like you, choose only to deal with a flesh and blood person.

My mortgage and loan repayments will, therefore and no longer be automatic, but will arrive at your bank, by cheque, addressed personally and confidentially to an employee of your branch, whom you must nominate. You will be aware that it is an offence under the Postal Act for any other person to open such an envelope.

Please find attached an Application For Contact Status which I require your chosen employee to complete. I am sorry it runs to eight pages, but in order that I know as much about him or her as your bank knows about me, there is no alternative.

Please note that all copies of his or her medical history must be countersigned by a Justice of the Peace, and that the mandatory details of his/her financial situation (income, debts, assets and liabilities) must be accompanied by documented proof.

In due course I will issue your employee with a PIN number, which he/she must quote in all dealings with me. I regret that it cannot be shorter than 28 digits but, again, I have modelled it on the number of button presses required to access my account balance on your phone bank service. As they say, imitation is the sincerest form of flattery.

Let me level the playing field even further by introducing you to my new telephone system, which you will notice, is very much like yours.

My Authorised Contact at your bank, the only person with whom I will have any dealings, may call me at any time and will be answered by an automated voice.

By pressing buttons on the phone, he/she will be guided thorough an extensive set of menus:
1. To make an appointment to see me;
2. To query a missing repayment;
3. To make a general complaint or inquiry;
4. To transfer the call to my living room in case I am there; Extension of living room to be communicated at the time the call is received;
5. To transfer the call to my bedroom case I am still sleeping. Extension of bed room to be communicated at the time the call is received;
6. To transfer the call to my toilet case I am attending to nature. Extension of toilet to be communicated at the time the call is received.
7. To transfer the call to my mobile phone in case I am not at home.
8. To leave a message on my computer. To leave a message a password to access my computer is required. Password will be communicated at a later date to the contact.

9. To return to the main menu and listen carefully to options 1 through 8.

The contact will then be put on hold, pending the attention of my automated answering service.

While this may on occasion involve a lengt hy wait, uplifting music will play for the duration. This month I've chosen a refrain from The Best Of Woody Guthrie:

Oh, the banks are made of marble

With a guard at every door

And the vaults are filled with silver

That the miners sweated for!

After twenty minutes of that, our mutual contact will probably know it off by heart. On a more serious note, we come to the matter of cost. As your bank has often pointed out, the ongoing drive for greater efficiency comes at a cost - a cost which you have always been quick to pass on to me. Let me repay our kindness by passing some costs back.

First, there is the matter of advertising material you send me. This I will read for a fee of $20 per A4 page. Inquiries from your nominated contact will be billed at $5 per minute of my time spent in response.

Any debits to my account, as, for example, in the matter of the penalty for the dishonoured cheque, will be passed back to you. My new phone service runs at 75 cents a minute (even Woody Guthrie doesn't come for free), so you would be well advised to keep your inquiries brief and to the point.

Regrettably, but again following your example, I must also levy an establishment fee to cover the setting up of this new arrangement.

May I wish you a happy, if ever-so-slightly less prosperous, New Year.

Your humble client.

Information

Airlines

All too rarely, airline attendants make an effort to make the in-flight safety lecture" and their other announcements a bit more entertaining.

Here are some examples that have been heard or reported: Enjoy!!

1. On a Continental Flight with a very "senior" flight attendant crew, the pilot said, "Ladies and gentlemen, we've reached cruising altitude and will be turning down the cabin lights. This is for your comfort and to enhance the appearance of your flight attendants."

****

2. On landing, the stewardess said, "Please be sure to take all of your belongings. If you're going to leave anything, please make sure it's something we'd like to have."

****

3. There may be 50 ways to leave your lover, but there are only 4 ways out of this airplane.

****

4. "Thank you for flying Delta Business Express. We hope you enjoyed giving us the business as much as we enjoyed taking you for a ride."

****

5. As the plane landed and was coming to a stop at La Guardia, a lone voice came over the loudspeaker: "Whoa, big fella. WHOA!"

****

6. After a particularly rough landing during thunderstorms in Memphis, a flight attendant on a Northwest flight announced, "Please take care when opening the overhead compartments because, after a landing like that, sure as hell everything has shifted."

****

7. From a Southwest Airlines employee: "Welcome aboard Southwest Flight 245 to Tampa. To operate your seat belt, insert the metal tab into the buckle, and pull tight. It works just like every other seat belt; and, if you don't know how to operate one, you probably shouldn't be out in public unsupervised.

****

8. In the event of a sudden loss of cabin pressure, masks will descend from the ceiling. Stop screaming, grab the mask, and pull it over your face. If you have a small child travelling with you, secure your mask before assisting with theirs. If you are travelling with more than one small child, pick your favourite.

9. Weather at our destination is 50 degrees with some broken clouds, but we'll try to have them fixed before we arrive. Thank you, and remember, nobody loves you, or your money, more than Southwest Airlines."

10. "Your seat cushions can be used for flotation; and, in the event of an emergency water landing, please paddle to shore and keep them with our compliments."

11. "Should the cabin lose pressure, oxygen masks are in the overhead area. Please place the bag over your own mouth and nose before assisting children… or other adults acting like children."

12. "As you exit the plane, make sure to gather all of your belongings. Anything left behind will be distributed evenly among the flight attendants. Please do not leave children or spouses."

13. And from the pilot during his welcome message: "Delta airlines is pleased to have some of the best flight attendants in the industry. Unfortunately, none of them are on this flight!"

14. Heard on Southwest Airlines just after a very hard landing in Salt Lake City: The flight attendant came on the intercom and said, "That

was quite a bump, and I know what y'all are thinking. I'm here to tell you it wasn't the airline's fault, it wasn't the pilot's fault, it wasn't the flight attendant's fault…..it was the asphalt."

****

15. Overheard on an American Airlines flight into Amarillo, Texas, on a particularly windy and bumpy day: During the final approach, the Captain was really having to fight it. After an extremely hard landing, the Flight Attendant said, "Ladies and Gentlemen, welcome to Amarillo. Please remain in your seats with your seat belts fastened while the Captain taxis what's left of our airplane to the gate!"

****

16. Another flight attendant's comment on a less than perfect landing: "We ask you to please remain seated as Captain Kangaroo bounces us to the terminal."

****

17. An airline pilot wrote that on this particular flight he had hammered his ship into the runway really hard. The airline had a policy which required the first officer to stand at the door while the Passengers exited, smile, and give them a "Thanks for flying our airline." He said that, in light of his bad landing, he had a hard time looking the passengers in the eye, thinking that someone would have a smart comment. Finally everyone had gotten

off except for a little old lady walking with a cane. She said, "Sir, do you mind if I ask you a question?" "Why, no, Ma'am," said the pilot. "What is it?" The little old lady said, "Did we land, or were we shot down?"

****

18. After a real crusher of a landing in Phoenix, the Flight Attendant came on with, "Ladies and Gentlemen, please remain in your seats until Capt. Crash and the Crew have brought the aircraft to a screeching halt against the gate. And, once the tire smoke has cleared and the warning bells are silenced, we'll open the door and you can pick your way through the wreckage to the terminal."

****

19. Part of a flight attendant's arrival announcement: "We'd like to thank you folks for flying with us today. And, the next time you get the insane urge to go blasting through the skies in a pressurized metal tube, we hope you'll think of US Airways."

****

20. A plane was taking off from Kennedy Airport. After it reached a comfortable cruising altitude, the captain made an announcement over the intercom, "Ladies and gentlemen, this is your captain speaking. Welcome to Flight Number 293, nonstop from New York to Los Angeles. The weather ahead is good and, therefore, we should have a smooth and uneventful flight.

Now sit back and relax… OH, MY GOD!" Silence followed, and after a few minutes, the captain came back on the intercom and said, "Ladies and Gentlemen, I am so sorry if I scared you earlier. While I was talking to you, the flight attendant brought me a cup of coffee and spilled the hot coffee in my lap. You should see the front of my pants!" A passenger in Coach yelled, "That's nothing. You should see the back of mine!"

Ingenuity

Cancel the crane – we've sorted it

Handsfree

IF ANYONE IS INTERESTED PLEASE LET ME KNOW ASAP AS THEY ARE SELLING QUICK…

I don't know if you've heard, but starting 1 December 2003, you will no longer be able to use a mobile phone while driving, unless you have a "hands free" adaptor.

I went to a Mobile Phone Shop and they wanted £50 for a headset with a boom microphone for my mobile phone. I have found an alternative from Staples that is compatible with any mobile phone and one size fits all. I paid £0.08 each for buying in quantity and I am selling them for £1.99 including postage.

I have tried these out on Ericsson, Motorola, & Nokia handsets and they worked perfectly.

A photo is attached - take a look and let me know if you want one.

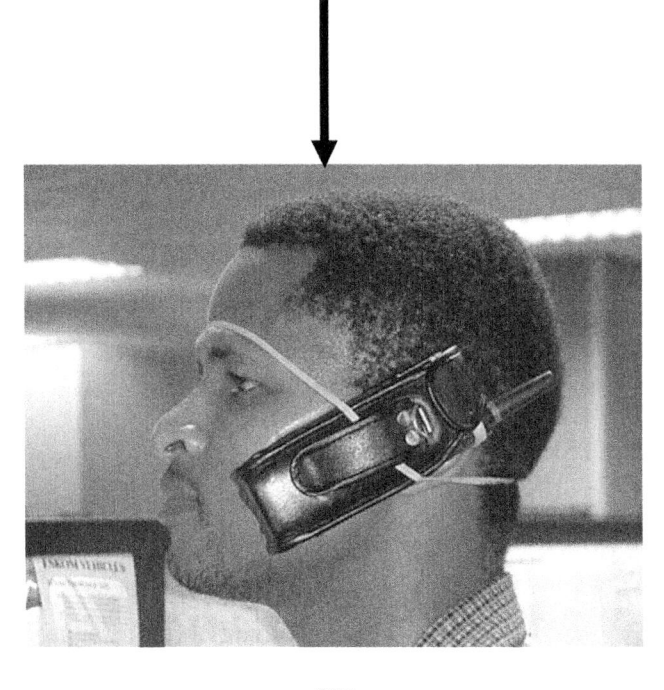

Watch out for this scam

Yesterday, one of my neighbours was car-hijacked at a traffic light!

A young woman proposes to wash your car window while you wait at the red light, and another one takes advantage of it to open the back door and steal everything she can grab. Be warned, they are very well organized!!!

Don't leave your doors or windows open if you drive up to a red light!

If your windows get washed .... Don't look at them, they try to distract you.

Please inform your friends of this new scam. They have gotten me 10 times already.

Advertising

A desperate Australian male

An ad found in the Canberra Times, Personals Section: This bloke should have got a few replies simply for taking the time to think of this!

Wanted
A tall well-built woman with good
reputation, who can cook chicken
legs, who appreciates a good fuc-
chia garden, classic music and talking without getting too serious.

Interested? Then please only read lines 1, 3 and 5; still interested?
Call me at...... (06) 2525 2037

Natural disasters

Dudley Earthquake appeal

URGENT - DUDLEY EARTHQUAKE APPEAL

At 00:54 on Monday 23 September an earthquake measuring 4.8 on the Richter scale hit Dudley, UK causing untold disruption and distress -

* Many were woken well before their giro arrived

* Several priceless collections of mementos from the Balearics and Spanish costas were damaged

* Three areas of historic and scientifically significant litter were disturbed

* Thousands are confused and bewildered, trying to come to terms with the fact that something interesting has happened in Dudley. One resident, Donna-Marie Dutton, a 17 year old mother-of-three said, "It was such a shock, little Chantal-Leanne came running into my bedroom crying. My youngest two, Tyler-Morgan and Megan-Storm slept through it. I was still shaking when I was watching Trisha the next morning."

Apparently though, looting did carry on as normal. The British Red Cross have so far managed to ship 4000 crates of Sunny Delight to the area to help the stricken masses. Rescue workers are still searching through the rubble and have found large quantities of personal belongings including benefit books and jewellery from Elizabeth Duke at Argos.

HOW YOU CAN HELP

* £2 buys chips, scraps and blue pop for a family of four

* £10 can take a family to Stourport for the day, where children can play on an unspoiled canal bank among the national collection of stinging nettles

* 22p buys a biro for filling in a spurious compensation claim

PLEASE ACT NOW

Simply email us by return with your credit card details and we'll do the rest! If you prefer to donate cash, there are collection points available at your local branches of Argos, Iceland and Clinton Cards.

Liverpool's worst air disaster occurred early this morning when a small two-seater Cessna plane crashed into a cemetery. Irish search and rescue workers have recovered 1826 bodies so far and expect that number to climb as digging continues into the night.

How to handle an irate customer

For all of you out there who've had to deal with an irate customer, this one is for you. It's a classic! In tribute to those "special" customers we all love! An award should go to the United Airlines gate agent in

Denver for being smart and funny, while making her point, when confronted with a passenger who probably deserved to fly as cargo.

A crowded United Airlines flight was cancelled. A single agent was rebooking a long line of inconvenienced travellers. Suddenly an angry passenger pushed his way to the desk. He slapped his ticket on the counter and said, "I HAVE to be on this flight and it has to be FIRST CLASS." The agent replied, "I am sorry, sir. I'll be happy to try to help you, but I've got to help these folks first, and I'm sure we'll be able to work something out."

The passenger was unimpressed. He asked loudly, so that the passengers behind him could hear, "DO YOU HAVE ANY IDEA WHO I AM?" Without hesitating, the agent smiled and grabbed her public address microphone, "May I have your attention please," she began her voice heard clearly throughout the terminal. "We have a passenger here at Gate 14 WHO DOES NOT KNOW WHO HE IS. If anyone can help him find his identity, please come to Gate 14."

With the folks behind him in line laughing hysterically, the man glared at the United agent, gritted his teeth and swore "Fuck You!" Without flinching, she smiled and said, "I'm sorry, sir, but you'll have to get in line for that too."

Answers to those every day questions

Q. What is the difference between a drug dealer and a hooker?
A. A hooker can wash her crack and sell it again.

Q. Why do women call it PMS?
A. Mad Cow Disease was already taken.

Q. What's the height of conceit?
A. Having an orgasm and calling out your own name.

Q. What's the definition of macho?
A. Jogging home from your own vasectomy.

Q. What's the difference between a G-Spot and a golf ball?
A. A guy will actually search for a golf ball.

Q. Do you know how people from Arkansas practice safe sex?
A. They spray paint X's on the back of the animals that kick.

Q. Why is divorce so expensive?
A. Because it's worth it.

Q. What is a Yankee?
A. The same as a quickie, but a guy can do it alone.

Q. What do Tupperware and a walrus have in common?
A. They both like a tight seal.

Q. What do a Christmas tree and priest have in common?
A. Their balls are just for decoration.

Q. What is the difference between "ooooooh" and "aaaaaaah"?
A. About three inches.

Q. What do you call a lesbian with fat fingers?
A. Well-hung.

Q. Why do gay men wear ribbed condoms?
A. For traction in the mud.

Q. What's the difference between purple and pink?
A. The grip.

Q. How do you find a Blind Man in a nudist colony?
A. It's not hard.

Q. How do you circumcise a hillbilly?
A. Kick his sister in the jaw.

Q. What's the difference between a girlfriend and a wife?
A. 45 lbs.

Q. What's the difference between a boyfriend and a husband?
A. 45 minutes

Q. Why do men find it difficult to make eye contact?
A. Breasts don't have eyes.

Q. If the dove is the bird of peace, what is the bird of true love?
A. The swallow.

Q. What is the difference between medium and rare?
A. Six inches is medium, eight inches is rare.

Q. Why do most women pay more attention to their appearance than improving their minds?

A. Because most men are stupid but few are blind.

Q. Why do women rub their eyes when they get up in the morning?

A. They don't have balls to scratch

Chain Letters

The First Worthwhile Chain Letter

This chain letter was developed by virile men in order to make their sex life even more fantastic. As opposed to normal chain letters, this one costs nothing, and you can only win.

Simply send this e-mail to 9 of your best friends who are just as virile as you. Then anaesthetize your wife/girlfriend, put her in a large carton (don't forget some ventilation holes), and send it to the person who is at the top of your list. Soon, your name will be at the top of the list, and you will receive 823,542 women through the post.

Statistically, among those women, will be at least:
- 0.5 miss worlds
- 2.5 models
- 463 wild nymphos
- 3,234 good-looking nymphos
- 20,198 who enjoy multiple orgasms
- 40,198 bi-sexual women

In total, that is 64,294 women who are simply hornier, less inhibited, and tastier than the grumpy old bag you posted off. And, best of all, your original package is guaranteed not to be one of those that come back to you.

DO NOT BREAK THIS CHAIN LETTER

One bloke for example who sent the letter to only 5 instead of 9 of his friends got his original bird back, still in the old dressing gown he sent her off in, with the same old migraine attack, and the accusatorial expression on her face. On the same day, the international supermodel he'd been living with since he sent off his old girlfriend moved out to live with his best friend (to whom he had not sent the chain letter.)

While I am sending this letter, the bloke that is in 6th place above me has already received 837 women and is lying in hospital suffering from exhaustion.

Outside his ward are 452 more packages.

YOU MUST BELIEVE THIS E-MAIL

This is a unique opportunity to achieve a totally satisfying sex life. No expensive meals out, no lengthy conversations about trivialities (that only interest women) just so that you can screw her. No obligations, no grumpy mother-in-law, and no unpleasant surprises like marriage or engagement.

Do not hesitate: send this letter today to 9 of your best friends.

PS Even when you have no girlfriend, you can send your vacuum cleaner.

PPS This letter can also be copied to women you know so that they can prepare themselves for the great adventure that they may soon undertake.

(Must dash, the post has just arrived.)

Language

The F word

We all know that the "F" word is strongly disapproved of socially. There have been only ten occasions in history when it is universally accepted that the "F" word was the only word that could have been used. These occasions were: -

"Scattered fucking showers…..My arse!" - Noah, 4314 BC

"How the f___ did you work that out?" - Pythagoras, 126 BC

"You want WHAT on the fucking ceiling?" - Michelangelo, 1566

"Look at all them fucking Indians!" - General George Custer, Little Big Horn, 1877

"Any fucking idiot could understand that." - Albert Einstein, 1915

"It does so fucking look like her!" - Pablo Picasso, 1926

"Where the f___ are we?" - Amelia Earhart, 1937

"What the f___ was that?" - Mayor of Hiroshima, 1945

"Aw c'mon. Who the fuck's going to find out?" - Bill Clinton, 1999

"Jesus Christ, I didn't think they'd get this fucking mad." - Osama bin Laden 2001

Spelling made easy

A bus stops and two Italian men get on. They sit down and engage in an animated conversation. The lady sitting behind them ignores them at first, but her attention is galvanized when she hears one of the men say the following:

"Emma come first. Den I come. Den two asses come together. I come once-a-more. Two asses, they come together again. I come again and pee twice. Then I come one lasta time."

"You foul-mouthed sex obsessed swine" retorted the lady indignantly. "In this country…we don't speak aloud in public places about our sex lives……..

"Hey, cooladown lady," said the man. "Who talkin' abouta sexa? I'm a just tellin' my friend how to spella 'Mississippi'."

I BET YOU READ THIS AGAIN!!!!

Complaints to the Council

1. These are extracts from actual letters sent to various councils and housing associations throughout the UK.. Enjoy!
2. I want some repairs done to my cooker as it has backfired and burnt my knob off.

THE GREATEST JOKE COMPENDIUM OF ALL TIME — FOR OUR TIMES

3. I wish to complain that my father hurt his ankle very badly when he put his foot in the hole in his back passage. Also their 18 year old son is continually banging his balls against my fence.
4. I wish to report that the tiles are missing from the outside toilet roof, I think it was that bad wind the other night that blew them off.
5. I am writing on behalf of my sink, which is coming away from the wall.
6. Will you please send someone to mend the garden path, my wife tripped and fell on it yesterday and now she is pregnant.
7. I request permission to remove my drawers in the kitchen. 50% of the walls are damp, 50% have crumbling plaster and the rest are plain filthy.
8. The toilet is blocked and we cannot bath the children until it is cleared.
9. Will you please send a man to look at my water; it is a funny colour and not fit to drink.
10. Our lavatory seat is broken in half and is now in three pieces.
11. I want to complain about the farmer across the road, every morning at 6am his cock wakes me up and its now getting too much for me.
12. The man next door has a large erection in the garden, which is unsightly and dangerous.
13. Our kitchen floor is damp. We have two small children and would like a third so please send someone round to do something about it.

14. I am a single women living in a downstairs flat and would you please do something about the noise made by the man I have on top of me every night.
15. Please send a man with the right tool to finish the job and satisfy my wife.
16. I have had the clerk of the works down on the floor six times but I still have had no satisfaction.
17. This is to let you know that our loo seat is broken and we can't get BBC2.
18. My bush is really overgrown round the front and my back passage has fungus in it.
19. He's got this huge tool that vibrates the whole house and I just can't take it anymore.

Footie

World cup 2006

Fast forward to 2006 - it is just before Scotland v Brazil at the next World Cup Group game. Ronaldo goes into the Brazilian changing room to find all his teammates looking a bit glum.

"What's up?" he asks.

"Well, we're having trouble getting motivated for this game. We know it's important but it's only Scotland. They're shite and we can't be bothered".

Ronaldo looks at them and says, "Well, I reckon I can beat these by myself, you lads go down the pub."

So Ronaldo goes out to play Scotland by himself and the rest of the Brazilian team go off for a few jars. After a few pints they wonder how the game is going, so they get the landlord to put the teletext on. A big cheer goes up as the screen reads "Brazil 1 - Scotland 0 (Ronaldo 10minutes)". He is beating Scotland all by himself!

Anyway, a few more pints later and the game is forgotten until someone remembers "It must be full time now, let's see how he got on". They put the teletext on.

"Result from the Stadium "Brazil 1(Ronaldo 10 minutes) - Scotland 1(Angus McShite 89minutes)".

They can't believe it, he has single handedly got a draw against Scotland! They rush back to the Stadium to congratulate him. They find him in the dressing room, still in his gear, sat with his head in his hands. He refuses to look at them. "I've let you down, I've let you down." "Don't be daft, you got a draw against Scotland, all by yourself. And they only scored at the very very end!"

"No, No, I have, I've let you down… I got sent off after 12 minutes"

World Cup 2006 – Squads announced!

The following squads have just been announced for the 2006 World Cup

BRAZILIAN SQUAD FOR WORLD CUP 2006
Pinnochio
Libero
Vimto
Memento
Borneo
Tango
Cheerio
Subbuteo
Scenario
Fellatio
Portfolio

SUBS:
Placebo
Porno
Polio
Banjo
Brasso
Stereo (L)
Stereo (r)
Hydrochlorofluoro
Aristotle

YUGOSLAVIAN SQUAD FOR WORLD CUP 2006
Itch
Annoyingitch
Hardtoreachitch
Scratchanitch
Hic
Sic
Spic
Pric
Digaditch
Fallinaditch
Horseraditch

SUBS:
Mowapitch
Letsgetrich
Shagabitch

RUSSIAN SQUAD FOR WORLD CUP 2006
Whodyanicabolicov

Ticlycov
Chesticov
Nasticov
Slalomsky
Downhillsky
Risky
Swedishshev
Mastershev
Fuckov
Taykitov

SUBS:
Rubitov
Gechakitov
Sodov
Pastryshev
Najinsky
Desert Orchid

ROMANIAN SQUAD FOR WORLD CUP 2006
Chatanoogaciouciou
Atishiou
Blessiou
Thankyiou
Busqueue
Snookercu
Pennyciou
Twoapennyciou
Fourapennyciou
I'llgetciou
Youandwhosarmi

SUBS:
U
NonU
ManU
Stuffyiou
Lee Kwan Yu

DANISH SQUAD FOR WORLD CUP 2006
Toomanigoalssen
Tryandstopussen
Crapdefenssen
Haveagossen
Firstsson
Seccondsson
Thirdsson
Legshurtssen
Notroubleseeingussen
Wherestheballssen
Getthebeerssen

SUBS:
Howmanygoalsisthatssen
Finallygaveupcountinssen
Hurryupandblowthewhistlessen
Yourelatedtoalexfergusonssen

ITALIAN SQUAD FOR WORLD CUP 2006
Baloni
Potbelli
Beerbelli
Giveitsumwelli

Wotsontelli
Toonsgotkenni
Onetoomani
Legslikejelli
Havabenni
Wobblijelli
Spendapenni

SUBS:
Cantthinkofani!!!
Buggermi

MEXICAN SQUAD FOR WORLD CUP 2006
San Francisco
Costa Brava
Hopelez
Juan Andonly
Manuel Gearbox Don
Criformi-Argentina
Bodegas
Luis Canon
Sombrero
Chihuahua
Taco Bell

SUBS:
Jesus Maria Don Key
Burrito
Speedy Gonzalez
Tequila
Caramba
Little Paco

DUTCH SQUAD FOR WORLD CUP 2006

Kenning van Hire
Van Diemansland
Van der Valk
Van Gard
Van Erealdizeez
Ad van Tagus
Hertz van Rental
Transit van Dors
Van Coova
Van Sprokendown
Aye van Hoe

SUBS:
Van Iller
Van Ishincreme
Van Morrison
Van Sectomy

News reaches us that Brazilian striker Fellatio no longer has a limp. This could prove to be a major blow. Two players who are not included are Russian hardman Sendimov, who will be serving a three-month suspension, and the hard-working Mexican midfielder, Manuel Labour. There is no place in the Dutch squad for sweeper, Dick van Dyke. The young Dutch star Per Vert has been excluded from the squad, after he was discovered in the back streets of Amsterdam with his finger in a dyke.

Dodgy Radio Interviews

Oz

A radio station in the Australia recently ran a phone-in competition to find the most embarrassing moments in listeners lives. The following are the final four place getters:

4th place

"While in line at the bank one afternoon, my toddler decided to release some pent-up energy and started to run amuck. I was finally able to grab hold of her after receiving looks of disgust and annoyance from other patrons.

I told her that if she didn't start behaving herself right now, she would be punished. To my horror, she looked me in the eye and said in a voice just as threatening, "If you don't let me go right now, I will tell Grandma that I saw you kissing Daddy's pee-pee last night!"

The silence was deafening, after this enlightening exchange. Even the tellers stopped what they were doing! I mustered the last of my dignity and walked out of the bank with my daughter in tow. The last thing that I heard as the door closed behind me were the screams of laughter."

3rd place

"It was the day before my 18th birthday. I was living at home, but my parents had gone out for the evening, so I invited my girlfriend over for a romantic night alone. As we lay in bed after making love, we heard the telephone ringing downstairs. I suggested to my girlfriend that I give her a piggyback ride to the phone. Since we didn't want to miss the call, we didn't have time to get dressed. When we got to the bottom of the stairs, the lights suddenly came on and a whole crowd of people yelled, "surprise". My entire family,… aunts, uncles, grandparents, cousins and all of my friends were standing there! My girlfriend and I were frozen to the spot in a state of shock and embarrassment for what seemed like an eternity. Since then, no one in my family has planned a surprise party again."

2nd place

"A lady picked up several items at a discount store. When she finally got up to the checkout, she learned that one of the items had no price tag. Imagine her embarrassment when the checker got on the public address system and boomed out for the entire store to hear. "PRICE CHECK ON LANE 13. TAMPAX, SUPERSIZE." That was bad enough, but somebody at the rear of the store apparently misunderstood the word "Tampax" for "Thumbtacks". In a very business-like tone, a voice boomed back over the public address system: DO YOU WANT THE KIND YOU PUSH IN

WITH YOUR THUMB OR THE KIND YOU BELT IN WITH A HAMMER?"

AND THE WINNER IS!

This one happened at a major Australian University in October last year. In a biology lecture, a professor was discussing the high glucose levels found in semen. A young female freshman, raised her hand and asked, If I understand what you are saying, there is a lot of glucose in male semen, as in sugar?" "That's correct," responded the professor, going on to add some statistical data. Raising her hand again, the girl asked, "Then why doesn't it taste sweet?" After a stunned silence, the whole class burst out laughing, the poor girl turned bright red and as she realised exactly what she had inadvertently said (or rather implied), she picked up her books, and without a word walked out of the class, and never returned. However, as she was going out of the door, the professor's reply was a classic. Totally straight-faced, he answered her question; "It doesn't taste sweet because the taste-buds for sweetness are on the tip of your tongue and not in the back of your throat!"

At work

Bad day at the office!

The teacher

THE TEACHER COMEBACK OF THE YEAR

A college teacher reminds her class of tomorrow's final exam. "Now class, I won't tolerate any excuses for you not being here tomorrow. I might consider a nuclear attack or a serious personal injury or illness, or a death in your immediate family but that's it, no other excuses whatsoever!"

A smart-ass guy in the back of the room raised his hand and asks, "What would you say if tomorrow I said I was suffering from complete and utter sexual exhaustion?"

The entire class does its best to stifle their laughter and snickering. When silence is restored, the teacher smiles sympathetically at the student, shakes her head, and sweetly says, "Well, I guess you'd have to write the exam with your other hand." HAHAHAHAHA…

Charity

An appeal

Dear All,

I don't normally make a habit of forwarding charity e-mails, but this seemed to be a particularly good cause. I know it touched me personally.

Mute Tourette's syndrome has long been in the shadow of its more famous sister-disease, 'Tourette's Syndrome', and although much rarer, is even more tragic in its consequences.

While a child suffering from Tourette's has difficulty in containing its anger and frustration, a child with Mute Tourette's suffers the opposite fate, and is unable to express their true feelings.

There is, however, an answer. A great deal has been achieved by the Mute Tourette's Foundation using new art therapy techniques.

However, their work can only continue with your help. Just £2.00 will keep a child supplied with crayons for a whole day. £5.00 will provide them with enough paper for a week.

Please give what you can to help this deserving cause.
Thank you

Technology

Wrong email address

After being nearly snowbound for two weeks last winter, a Seattle man departed for his vacation in Miami Beach, where he was to meet his wife them next day at the conclusion of her business trip to Minneapolis. They were looking forward to pleasant weather and a nice time together. Unfortunately, there was some sort of mix up at the boarding gate, and the man was told he would have to wait for a later flight. He tried to appeal to a supervisor but was told the airline was not responsible for the problem and it would do no good to complain.

Upon arrival at the hotel the next day, he discovered that Miami Beach was having a heat wave, and its weather was almost as uncomfortably hot as Seattle's was cold. The desk clerk gave him a message that his wife would arrive as planned. He could hardly wait to get to the pool area to cool off, and quickly sent his wife an e-mail, but due to his haste, he made an error in the e-mail address.

His message therefore arrived at the home of an elderly preacher's wife whose even older husband had died only the day before.

When the grieving widow opened her e-mail, she took one look at the monitor, let out an anguished scream, and fell to the floor dead.

Her family rushed to her room where they saw this message on the screen: Dearest wife, departed yesterday as you know. Just now got checked in. Some confusion at the gate. Appeal was denied. Received confirmation of your arrival tomorrow. Your loving husband.

P.S. Things are not as we thought. You're going to be surprised at how hot it is down here.

Christmas

Do you believe?

It is Christmas Eve and this chap is on a rooftop about to jump off.

His wife is leaving him for another man, he has lost his job and he owes thousands of pounds to the bank.

Just as he finishes his prayers and closes his eyes, ready to jump, Father Christmas taps him on the shoulder. "Are you OK?" asks Father Christmas. The man explains why he is so miserable and gets ready to jump.

"Stop!" shouts Father Christmas. "It is Christmas, I will grant you three wishes to solve your problems on the understanding that you will >grant me a small favour in return!" "Would you?" the man replies. "That would be wonderful!!... Thank you, thank you!"

Father Christmas promises him that:
1. You shall go home in 1 hour and your wife will be dressed in her sexiest underwear, begging for forgiveness and longing for your return.

She will have no recollection of her new boyfriend.
2. You shall go into work tomorrow, sit at your desk and continue with your work. Your salary will have increased by 50%. Also, nobody will have any recollection of your sacking.
3. You shall go to your bank and you will be ten thousand pounds in credit, you will have no outstanding bills.

"Oh thank you, thank you!" says the man. "What is it that I can do for you?"

Father Christmas asks the man to drop his pants and bend over.

After a quite brutal Rogering, which made his eyes water a little, Father Christmas asks the man how old he is.

36" replies the man.

Ho, Ho, Ho, You're a bit old to believe in Father Christmas aren't you?"

Pure Genius

Is Hell exothermic (gives off heat) or endothermic (absorbs heat)?

Most students wrote proofs of their beliefs using Boyle's Law, (gas cools as it expands and heats up when it is compressed) or some variant. One student however, wrote the following:

First, we need to know how the mass of Hell is changing in time. So we need to know the rate that souls are moving into Hell and the rate they are leaving. I think we can safely assume that once a soul gets to Hell it will not leave. Therefore, no souls are leaving.

As for how many souls are entering Hell, lets look at the different religions that exist in the world today. Some of these religions state that if you are not a member of their religion, you will go to Hell. Since there are more than one of these religions and since people do not belong to more than one religion, we can project that all souls go to Hell.

With birth and death rates as they are we can expect the number of souls in Hell to increase exponentially.

Now, we look at the rate of change of the volume of Hell because Boyle's Law states that in order for the temperature and pressure to stay the same, the volume of Hell has to expand as souls are added.

This gives two possibilities:

If Hell is expanding at a slower rate than the rate at which souls enter Hell, then the temperature and pressure in Hell will increase until all Hell breaks loose.

If Hell is expanding at a faster rate than the rate at which souls enter Hell, then the temperature and pressure will drop until Hell freezes over.

So which is it?

If we accept the postulate given to me by Ms. Banyan during my freshman year that, 'It will be a cold day in Hell before I sleep with you' and we take into account the fact that I have not succeeded in having sexual relations with her, then #2 cannot be true.

Thus I am sure that Hell is exothermic and will not freeze.

The student received the only 'A' given

Maths Exam

For the unaware, there is a slight difference between private schools and comprehensives in Britain. The Department of Education has realised this and has revised the secondary Maths Exam papers accordingly.

Attached are the most recent maths exam papers for your reference.

THE GREATEST JOKE COMPENDIUM OF ALL TIME — FOR OUR TIMES

MATHS TEST FOR COMPREHENSIVES
Name _____
Nickname _____
Gang Name _____

1. Simon has 0.5 kilos of cocaine. If he sells an 8 ball to Matt for 300 quid and 90 grams to Ollie for 90 quid a gram, what is the street value of the rest of his hold?
2. Damon pimps 3 bitches. If the price is GBP40 a ride, how many jobs per day must each bitch perform to support Damon's GBP500 a day coke habit?
3. Crackster wants to cut the kilo of cocaine he bought for 7,000 quid, to make a 20% profit. How many grams of ammonia will he need?
4. Trev got 6 years for murder. He also got 350,000 for the hit. If his common law wife spends 33,100 per month, how much money will be left when he gets out? Extra Credit Bonus: How much more time will Trev get for killing the slapper that spent his money?
5. If an average can of spray paint covers 22 square meters and the average letter is 1 square meter, how many letters can be sprayed with eight fluid ounce cans of spray paint with 20% extra paint free?
6. Liam steals Jordan's skateboard. As Liam skates away at a speed of 35mph, Jordan loads his brother's Armalite. If it takes Jordan 20 seconds to load the gun, how far will Liam have travelled when he gets whacked?

MATHS TEST FOR PRIVATE SCHOOLS
Name_____
_____
_____
(If longer, please continue on separate sheet)
School _____
Daddy's Company _____

1. Tarquin smashes up the old man's car, causing x amount of damage and killing three people. The old man asks his local CC to intervene in the court system, then forges his insurance claim and receives a payment of y. The difference between x and y is three times the life insurance settlement for the three dead people. What kind of car is Tarquin driving now?

2. Fiona's personal shopper decides to substitute generic and own-brand products for the designer goods favoured by her employer. In the course of a month she saves the price of a return ticket to Fiji and Fiona doesn't even notice the difference. Is she thick or what?

3. Tristram fancies the arse off a certain number of tarts, but he only has enough Rohypnol left to render 33.3% unconscious. If he has 14 Rohypnol, how is he ever going to shag the other two-thirds?

4. Henry is unsure about his sexuality. Three days a week he fancies women. On the other days he fancies men, ducks and vacuum cleaners. However, he only has access to the Hoover

every third week. When does his Sunday Independent column start?

Bush reasoning

President Bush and Colin Powell are sitting in a bar. A guy walks in and asks the barman, "Isn't that Bush and Powell sitting over there?"

The barman says, "Yep, that's them."

So the guy walks over and says, "Wow, this is a real honour. What are you guys doing in here?"

Bush says, "We're planning WW I I I ".

And the guy says, "Really? What's going to happen?"

Bush says, "Well, we're going to kill 140 million Iraqis this time and one bicycle repairman."

The guy exclaimed, "A bicycle repairman? Why kill a bicycle repairman?" Bush turns to Powell, punches him on the shoulder and says, "See, smart ass! I told you no one would worry about the 140 million Iraqis!"

Kylie

Alone at last

A passenger plane travelling to California is suddenly hit with a severe engine problem and plummets into the Pacific Ocean. The impact is such that the plane is ripped apart leaving only one man alive. After hours of swimming he spies an island and drags himself up onto the sandy shores. Though he is half drowned and aware that he is thousands of miles from home, he cannot but admire the beauty of the island he has found himself on.

Looking down the beach he sees a figure lying on the beach, another survivor from the crash. He runs over and sees that she is not breathing, so quickly he gives her the kiss of life.

After several attempts she coughs into life. As she wipes the hair from her face he now can see who it is…………………it's Kylie Minogue. Forever grateful to him for saving her life, they strike up an immediate bond, and over the following weeks, while stranded on the island, they fall madly in love. One day Kylie is walking down the beach and notices her new found Love sitting on the rocks by the beach, staring out to sea, with a look of sorrow on his face. She wanders over to him, and asks what is wrong.

"Kylie," he says, "The last few weeks have been the greatest of my life. We've found this island paradise. We have all the food and water we could require, and I have you, but still I can't help feel there's something missing." Kylie replies: "What my darling? What is it that you need? I'll do anything".

"Well there is one thing. Would you mind putting on my shirt?"

"OK"

"And my trousers?"

"OK"

At this point he gets up and grabs some charcoal from the ground, and draws a neat moustache on her lips.

"OK....... Can you start to walk around the island, and I'll set off the other way and meet you half way."

"OK dear, whatever will make you happy." So off they set. After an hour walking he eventually sees her heading towards him along the beach, at which point he breaks into a sprint, runs up to her, grabs her by the shoulders and shouts:

"Hey mate, you won't f**king believe who I'm shagging!!

Still Bored??

Try This

BE WARNED: This is going to drive you crazy!

While sitting at your desk, lift your right foot off the floor and make clockwise circles.

Now, while doing this, draw the number "6" in the air with your right hand.

Your foot will change direction.

About the Author

Roy Vega is a professional who has worked in a number of roles in both the public and private sectors. In so doing he has met a wide variety of people and encountered a myriad of bygone situations.

Throughout his career Roy has constantly used humor to manage any situation and to make a difference to everyone he has met. As a result he has acquired a vast amount of material all of which he has been sent during the course of his work by like minded individuals.

The Compendium contains a selection of the best material broken back across all sections of community. This book will make you cry with laughter as well as recognize the behaviors of young and those around you by putting day to day into contrast!

Printed in Great Britain
by Amazon